Collins

11+
Stretch &
Challenge
Activities & Tests

Phil Marchant, Shelley Welsh
and Beatrix Woodhead

Acknowledgements

Published by Collins
An imprint of HarperCollins*Publishers*
1 London Bridge Street
London SE1 9GF

HarperCollins*Publishers*
1st Floor, Watermarque Building,
Ringsend Road, Dublin 4, Ireland

ISBN: 978-0-00-848394-4

First published 2021

10 9 8 7 6 5 4 3 2 1

British Library Cataloguing in Publication Data.

A CIP record of this book is available from the British Library.

Publishers: Sundus Pasha and Clare Souza
Authors: Phil Marchant, Shelley Welsh and Beatrix Woodhead
With thanks to Chris Pearse at Teachitright for additional authoring and support
Project Management: Richard Toms
Cover Design: Sarah Duxbury
Inside Concept Design: Ian Wrigley
Typesetting and artwork: Jouve India Private Limited
Production: Karen Nulty
Printed in the United Kingdom by Martins the Printers

MIX
Paper from
responsible sources
FSC™ C007454

FSC
www.fsc.org

This book is produced from independently certified FSC™ paper to ensure responsible forest management.

For more information visit:
www.harpercollins.co.uk/green

Challenge 3

a) Plot the coordinates C (3, 6) and D (6, 6) on the grid to make a square.

b) Translate the square by (2, 2).

What are the new coordinates of point C? _____ 4,8

c) Plot the point E at (5, 0) to make the triangle ABE. Now draw a horizontal line from (0, 3) to (9, 3).

d) Reflect the triangle ABE in the horizontal line.

What are the new coordinates of point E after the reflection? _____

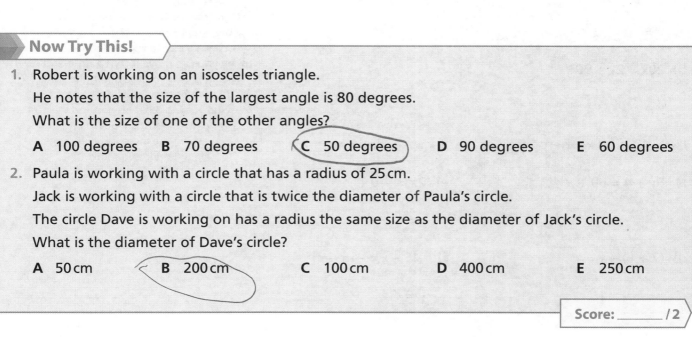

Score: _____ / 4

Challenge 4

a) Which 3D shape has 4 triangular faces, 1 square face, 8 edges and 5 vertices?

_____ square-based pyramid

b) Which 3D shape has 2 faces, 1 edge and 1 vertex?

_____ Cone

Score: _____ / 2

Now Try This!

1. Robert is working on an isosceles triangle.
   He notes that the size of the largest angle is 80 degrees.
   What is the size of one of the other angles?
   A 100 degrees   B 70 degrees   C 50 degrees   D 90 degrees   E 60 degrees

2. Paula is working with a circle that has a radius of 25 cm.
   Jack is working with a circle that is twice the diameter of Paula's circle.
   The circle Dave is working on has a radius the same size as the diameter of Jack's circle.
   What is the diameter of Dave's circle?
   A 50 cm   B 200 cm   C 100 cm   D 400 cm   E 250 cm

Score: _____ / 2

Total score _____ / 13

LOW   CONFIDENCE   HIGH

Mathematics   21

Let's Get S-t-r-e-t-c-h-i-n-g!

Algebra is maths with symbols instead of numbers. It helps us to find unknown values.

If $y + 4 = 6$, then we can work out that $y = 2$.

Challenge 1

a) Solve for y when $y + 16 = 29$

$y = $ _____

b) Find x when $4x = 16$

$x = $ _____

c) Find x when $7x - 49 = 0$

$x = $ _____

d) Find y when $\dfrac{125}{y} = 25$

$y = $ _____

e) Find y when $16y + 40 = 20y$

$y = $ _____

f) Find x when $40x + 400 = x + 985$

$x = $ _____

Score: _____ / 6

Challenge 2

If $x = 9$, find y when:

a) $7x + y = 85$

$y = $ _____

b) $20x = 2y + 90$

$y = $ _____

If $y = 12$, find x when:

c) $8y + 4 = 50 + x$

$x = $ _____

d) $(7 + y) - x = 1$

$x = $ _____

If $x = -4$, find y when:

e) $2x = -10 + y$

$y = $ _____

f) $-15 - x = -16 - y$

$y = $ _____

Problem Solving

Remember to solve equations by moving values either side of the equals sign. So if, for example, you have a +25 to the left of the equals sign, you can move it to the right and it becomes −25. You are doing the same thing to both sides of the equation (subtracting 25). This method will help you to break down and solve the more difficult algebraic equations.

Score: _____ / 6

Challenge 3

a) Solve x when:

$17x - 22 = 5x + 50$

$x =$ _____

b) Solve y when:

$14y^2 = 56$

$y =$ _____

c) Solve x when:

$\frac{50}{x} = 2x$

$x =$ _____

d) Solve y when:

$20y^2 = 20$

$y =$ _____

Score: _____ /4

Challenge 4

Find the value of y if x = 2 in these equations:

a) $3 + 2x(y + 1) = 27$

$y =$ _____

b) $29 + 3x(y + 7) = 77$

$y =$ _____

Find the value of y if x = 9 in these equations:

c) $16x + 16 + 9y = 190 - y$

$y =$ _____

d) $(x^2 + 25) + 2y = 133 - y$

$y =$ _____

Top Tip

Take care when you are multiplying expressions with brackets. For example, $3x(y + 2)$ means you multiply 3x by both y and the 2, so you get $3xy + 6x$.

Score: _____ /4

Now Try This!

1. Ahmed is working with this square.
   The square has a width of 4y + 2 cm.

   4y + 2 cm

   What is the perimeter of the square in centimetres?

   A $24y + 12$ B $16y + 4$ C $16y + 2$ D $8y + 8$ E $16y + 8$

2. Jenny is working on a rectangle that has a width of 3x + y cm and a length of 5x + 2y cm.
   What is the perimeter of the rectangle in centimetres?

   A $16x + 6y$ B $15x + 2y$ C $32x + 12y$ D $16x + 12y$ E $16x + 2y$

Score: _____ /2

Total score _____ /22

LOW   CONFIDENCE   HIGH

Mathematics   23

Let's Get S-t-r-e-t-c-h-i-n-g!

When you have two unknown values and two equations relating to them, you have simultaneous equations. So if you know that $3x + 2y = 13$ and that $x + 5y = 13$, you can solve to find x and y.

Problem Solving

With simultaneous equations, you need to get yourself in a position where you can find one value. You can do this by getting one of the equations in a form that means you can subtract the other. You can then substitute that value into the original equations to work out the other value.

In the example above left, multiplying the second equation by 3 gives $3x + 15y = 39$. Now you can subtract the first equation to remove the x to obtain $13y = 26$, $y = 2$. Substitute into the original equation: $3x + 2(2) = 13$, $3x + 4 = 13$, $3x = 9$, $x = 3$. So $x = 3$ and $y = 2$.

Challenge 1

a) I buy 3 rubbers and 2 pencils from a shop. The total cost is £1.90.

   If the rubbers are 50p each, how much does one pencil cost? ....

b) At a fast-food stall, I buy 3 hot dogs and 2 hamburgers for a total cost of £9.

   Write an expression for x and y, where x is the price of a hot dog and y is the price of a hamburger. ....

c) At another fast-food bar, a customer buys 4 portions of chips and 3 burgers at a total cost of £6.50.

   If a burger costs £1.50, how much is a portion of chips? ....

d) Multiply the equation $7x = 3.50$ by 2. What do you get? ....

Score: _____ / 4

Challenge 2

a) Find y where: $4y + x = 38$

                        $x = 6$

   $y =$ ....

b) Find y where: $9y + 2x = 120$

                        $x = 15$

   $y =$ ....

c) Find y where: $17y + 3x = 62$

                        $x = 15$

   $y =$ ....

d) Find y where: $300 - y - 3x = 90$

                        $x = 50$

   $y =$ ....

Score: _____ / 4

Challenge 3

a) Multiply these equations by 2:

   i) $3x + 8y = 2.50$ _____

   ii) $4x + y = 7.25$ _____

b) Multiply these equations by 3:

   i) $7y + 2x = 3$ _____

   ii) $y + 9x = 14$ _____

c) Subtract the bottom equation from the top:

$4y + 7x = 5.50$

$4y + 3x = 3.00$

_____

d) Subtract the top equation from the bottom:

$12y + 6x = 27$

$20y + 10x = 45$

_____

Score: _____ / 6

Challenge 4

Solve these simultaneous equations for x and y.

a) $4x + 2y = 5$

   $2x + 3y = 3.50$

      $x =$ _____ $y =$ _____

b) $3x + 2y = 4.90$

   $4x + 4y = 8.20$

      $x =$ _____ $y =$ _____

c) $3x + 4y = 8.35$

   $5x + 2y = 7.85$

      $x =$ _____ $y =$ _____

Score: _____ / 6

Now Try This!

1. Karim goes to a shop and buys 3 envelopes and 5 pens for £3.80.
   His friend goes to the same shop and buys 6 envelopes and 4 pens for £5.20.
   How much does 1 envelope cost in the shop?

   A 40p   **B** 50p   **C** 70p   **D** 60p   **E** 65p

2. In a supermarket, a customer buys 4 kitchen rolls and 3 cheese slices for £4.10.
   Another customer buys 3 kitchen rolls and 6 cheese slices for £5.70.
   How much does 1 kitchen roll cost in the supermarket?

   A 70p   **B** 50p   **C** 40p   **D** 60p   **E** 55p

Score: _____ / 2

Total score _____ / 22

LOW   CONFIDENCE   HIGH

Let's Get S-t-r-e-t-c-h-i-n-g!

The mean, median, mode and range are values that help us to understand data better:

- The mean is the average value.
- The median is the middle value when the data is ordered.
- The mode is the value that occurs most often.
- The range is the difference between the highest and the lowest values in the data.

Challenge 1

Consider these numbers: | 8 | 11 | 8 | 16 | 17 |

a) What is the mean of the numbers? ....

b) What is the mode of the numbers? ....

c) What is the range of the numbers? ....

d) What is the median of the numbers? ....

e) Consider the highest number in the list.

What number would you need to change this to
in order to make the new range of the numbers 22? ....

Score: _____ /5

Challenge 2

Consider these numbers: | 9 | 0 | 0 | 24 | 12 | 21 |

a) What is the mode of the numbers? ....

b) What is the mean of the numbers? ....

c) What is the median of the numbers? ....

d) What is the range of the numbers? ....

Now double the highest number in the box and answer these questions:

e) What is the mean of the numbers now? ....

f) What is the range of the numbers now? ....

g) What is the median of the numbers now? ....

Problem Solving

If you are presented with an even number of values, you find the median by taking the average of the two middle values when the data is arranged in order.

Score: _____ /7

Challenge 3

Five friends counted how many stickers they owned and the results are shown in this bar chart:

Number of stickers (bar chart: Mo 20, John 25, Dave 15, Ritu 10, Lucy 20)

Top Tip

You will often be presented with data in graphical form, such as a bar or a pie chart. Work through the chart to reveal the numbers and calculate the mean, median, mode and range from there.

a) What was the mode number of stickers? _____

b) What was the median number of stickers? _____

c) What was the range in the number of stickers? _____

d) What was the mean number of stickers? _____

Score: _____ / 4

Challenge 4

Sid has a set of number cards:

| 3 | 9 | 5 | 3 | 10 |

a) What is the range in the numbers on his cards? _____

b) Add the mode, median and mean numbers of all the cards.

What is the total? _____

Score: _____ / 2

Now Try This!

1. Carrie scored 64, 58, 66, 49, 58 and 74 in her first six exams.
   After the seventh and last exam, she had a mean result of 64 across all her exams.
   What score did she get in her last exam?

   A 79   B 78   C 80   D 76   E 82

2. The values a, b and c have a mode of 15 and a mean of 13.
   a is the lowest value.
   What is the value of $a + b$?

   A 20   B 19   C 25   D 22   E 24

Score: _____ / 2

Total score _____ / 20

LOW   CONFIDENCE   HIGH

Let's Get S-t-r-e-t-c-h-i-n-g!

Statistics questions in the 11+ test will require you to understand line graphs and pie charts and interpret them fully.

Challenge 1

Kieran has plotted the number of achievement points he gained at school each day on this graph.

a) Join up the points to make a line graph.

b) What was the total number of achievement points Kieran got across the three days?

_____

c) What was the range in the number of achievement points he got?

_____

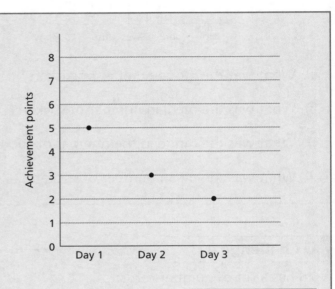

Score: _____ / 3

Challenge 2

Draw a line graph to show this data:

Day	Temperature (°C)
Monday	−2
Tuesday	4
Wednesday	7
Thursday	−1
Friday	0

Score: _____ / 6

Challenge 3

Sasha is using this data table in order to create a pie chart of the colours of crayons she owns.
Fill in the gaps in the table.

Colour	Number	Size of pie chart angle
Red	25	90 degrees
Blue		180 degrees
Green		90 degrees

Challenge 4

A group of pupils were asked which sport they played in the summer.
The results are recorded in this pie chart:

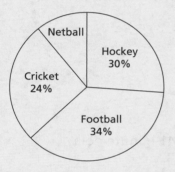

Problem Solving

You could be shown graphs or data that is incomplete. The information provided will always give you the tools to find out the missing data.

a) 48 pupils said they played cricket.

How many pupils said they played netball? ....

b) What was the total number of pupils that were asked? ....

Now Try This!

1. Three-fifths of the people on a train are looking at their phone.

    Of the remainder, one half are reading and the other half are looking out of the window.

    If you were presenting this information in a pie chart, what angle size would you use to represent the people looking out of the window?

    A 60 degrees   **B** 90 degrees   **C** 72 degrees   **D** 75 degrees   **E** 65 degrees

2. 240 people own a pet. 120 people do not.

    If you were presenting this information in a pie chart, what angle size would you use to represent the people who own a pet?

    A 260 degrees   **B** 220 degrees   **C** 250 degrees   **D** 240 degrees   **E** 200 degrees

Total score _____ / 15

LOW   CONFIDENCE   HIGH

Mathematics > Mixed Activities

1. a) What is the lowest common multiple of 14 and 10? (1)

   b) What is the highest common factor of 14 and 8? (1)

2. Liam is looking at his train timetable:

Southampton	14:28
London	15:47
Birmingham	17:36
Newcastle	19:56

   a) Liam gets on the train at Southampton and leaves it at Birmingham.

   How long does he spend on the train? (1)

   b) Liam's friend gets on the train at Birmingham. However, it suffers a 41-minute delay.

   What time does his friend arrive at Newcastle? (1)

3. This chart shows how far various towns are from London in miles.

London

54	Town A			
72	43	Town B		
38	39	63	Town C	
63	54	71	38	Town D

Problem Solving

Timetables for trains, trams or buses often appear in 11+ test questions. Make sure you can read them and understand any manipulation of the time or places that you are asked about.

   a) Which town is furthest from London? (1)

   b) How far is Town D from Town B? (1)

   c) How much closer is Town B to Town A than Town D is to Town A? (1)

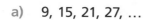
4. Find the next number in each of these sequences.

a) 9, 15, 21, 27, … (1)

_____

b) 7, 13, 20, 33, 53, … (1)

_____

c) 2, 12, 5, 24, 8, 48, … (1)

_____

Problem Solving

With number sequences, work out the pattern between the numbers. Look out for Fibonacci (adding the two previous numbers), prime numbers and square numbers. You may even find sequences where there are two patterns: one for the numbers in positions 1, 3, 5, 7 and one for those in positions 2, 4, 6, 8.

5. Triangle ABC has been plotted on the graph grid below.

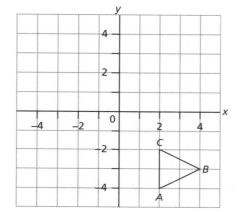

a) What are the coordinates of point C? (1)

(_____ , _____)

b) Reflect the triangle in the y axis.

What are the new coordinates of point B? (1)

(_____ , _____)

6. Ritu ran for 24 minutes at 10 kilometres per hour and then for 12 minutes at 5 kilometres per hour.

How far did she run in total? (1)

_____

7. Think about the hands on the face of a clock.

    a) What is the angle between two clock hands at 6:00?   (1)

    _____

    b) What is the angle between two clock hands at 3:30?
        Think about where the hour hand will be.   (1)

    _____

8. Triangle *ABC* has been drawn on the graph grid below.

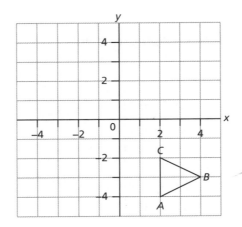

    a) Rotate the triangle around point *C* by 180 degrees.

        What are the new coordinates of point *B*?   (1)

        (_____ , _____)

    b) Using the graph above, draw a diagonal line where *x = y*.
        Reflect the triangle *ABC* in this line.

        What are the new coordinates of point *C*?   (1)

        (_____ , _____)

    Problem Solving

    With coordinates questions, make sure you know how to translate, reflect and rotate shapes. Reflections can also be through diagonal lines.

9. Sam leaves his house at 7:30 am.
    He travels at an average speed of 5 mph and reaches school at 7:45 am.

    How far is it from Sam's house to his school?   (1)

    _____

10. Annabelle is tossing a fair coin.

    What is the probability that it lands on the Heads side twice in a row?
    Give your answer as a fraction.   (1)

    ....

11. Give all your answers as percentages.

    Jim writes all the numbers from 1–20 on 20 different number cards.
    He then puts the cards in a bag.

    a)   If he picks out one card at random, what is the probability it will be an even number?   (1)

         ....

    b)   What is the probability that Jim will pull out a number that is a factor of 20?   (1)

         ....

    c)   What is the probability that Jim will pull out a square number?   (1)

         ....

    d)   What is the probability that Jim will pull out a prime number?   (1)

         ....

12. Think about the points of a compass.

    a)   Carole is facing due North. She turns by 90 degrees anticlockwise.

         In which direction is she now facing?   (1)

         ....

    b)   Moeen is facing exactly North West. He turns by 180 degrees clockwise.

         In which direction is he now facing?   (1)

         ....

> **Top Tip**
> Learn all the points
> of a compass and at what
> angle they are pointing.
> There are lots of mnemonics
> for remembering these.
> For example: Never Eat
> Soggy Waffles!

Total score _____ / 25

LOW   CONFIDENCE   HIGH

Mathematics   33

Let's Get S-t-r-e-t-c-h-i-n-g!

An author might use several different techniques to create a particular atmosphere. In comprehension test questions, you are often asked to consider:

- what type of atmosphere has been created
- how that atmosphere has been created
- how a setting or the author's choice of language can contribute in creating a particular feeling or response in a reader.

Top Tip

What effect does the setting, tone and mood have on you when you read a story? When you write a story yourself, try to create a particular atmosphere in order to make your reader feel a certain way.

Top Tip

An atmosphere is a feeling or mood created by the words of the story. Authors work hard to create and sustain an appropriate atmosphere throughout their stories because it helps the reader to feel immersed in the narrative.

Challenge 1

Read the extract below and answer the questions that follow on a separate piece of paper.

Like bees swarming after their queen, mother and daughters hovered about Mr. March the next day, neglecting everything to look at, wait upon, and listen to the new invalid, who was in a fair way to be killed by kindness. As he sat propped up in a big chair by Beth's sofa, with the other three close by, and Hannah popping in her head now and then 'to peek at the dear man', nothing seemed needed to complete their happiness. But something was needed, and the elder ones felt it, though none confessed the fact. Mr. and Mrs. March looked at one another with an anxious expression, as their eyes followed Meg.

From *Little Women*, by L M Alcott

a) How has the author created a vivid atmosphere in the extract? You might want to think about language choice, imagery, simile and metaphor. (3)

b) How has the author created tension through the use of contrast? (3)

Score: _____ / 6

Challenge 2

Read the extract below and answer the questions that follow on a separate piece of paper.

The end of the cylinder was being screwed out from within. Nearly two feet of shining screw projected. Somebody blundered against me, and I narrowly missed being pitched onto the top of the screw. I turned, and as I did so the screw must have come out, for the lid of the cylinder fell upon the gravel with a ringing concussion. I stuck my elbow into the person behind me, and turned my head towards the Thing again. For a moment that circular cavity seemed perfectly black. I had the sunset in my eyes.

From *The War of the Worlds*, by H G Wells

Problem Solving

Comprehension texts will sometimes come from books written many years ago. Therefore the speech and sentence structure may be different to what you are used to. You need to try to unpick the meaning of what you read.

a) What atmosphere has the writer created in this extract? How have they created a vivid image of the events? (3)

b) What do you think 'the Thing' is? Explain your answer. (3)

Score: _____ / 6

Challenge 3

a) Underline the interesting vocabulary that has contributed to the atmosphere in this piece of writing. For each, think about what the word makes you imagine. (3)

> The stranger came early in February, one wintry day, through a biting wind and a driving snow, the last snowfall of the year, over the down, walking from Bramblehurst railway station, and carrying a little black portmanteau in his thickly gloved hand. He was wrapped up from head to foot, and the brim of his soft felt hat hid every inch of his face but the shiny tip of his nose; the snow had piled itself against his shoulders and chest, and added a white crest to the burden he carried. He staggered into the "Coach and Horses" more dead than alive, and flung his portmanteau down.
>
> From *The Invisible Man*, by H G Wells

b) Overall, how would you describe the setting? Ominous? Spooky? Bleak? Write your ideas on a separate piece of paper. (2)

Score: _____ /5

Challenge 4

These boxes show some ideas for atmospheres that an author could try to create in their writing.

| Spooky | Jovial | Suspenseful |

| Light-hearted | Tense |

a) In the boxes below, write three other atmospheres that might be created in a text. (3)

b) On a separate piece of paper, write a story or a descriptive piece with any of the atmospheres given above or identified in part a). (15)

Score: _____ /18

Now Try This!

Read the extract below and answer the question that follows.

Top Tip

Description of the setting and of *how* the characters speak or move helps to establish the tone and atmosphere of a text.

> The intense interest aroused in the public by what was known at the time as "The Styles Case" has now somewhat subsided. Nevertheless, in view of the world-wide notoriety which attended it, I have been asked, both by my friend Poirot and the family themselves, to write an account of the whole story. This, we trust, will effectually silence the sensational rumours which still persist.
>
> From *The Mysterious Affair at Styles*, by Agatha Christie

What do we learn of "The Styles Case" in this extract?
A   It is an exciting piece of fiction
B   Members of the public have made up their own minds
C   There is much scandal as it is a tantalising story
D   Everyone wants to read a novel about it
E   The case follows a great detective

Score: _____ /1

Total score _____ /36

LOW   CONFIDENCE   HIGH

Let's Get S-t-r-e-t-c-h-i-n-g!

The characters are often vital to our enjoyment of literature. Remember to think about why characters are behaving in a particular way. Think about them as people with real opinions, feelings and responses.

Top Tip

While reading, you will likely come across unfamiliar vocabulary. Make a list of new words as you spot them. Try not to panic if a comprehension question asks you to define a word you do not know – you can use the context of the story around it to help you work out a sensible answer.

Top Tip

Don't forget to read poetry and short stories as well as novels and non-fiction. They are often forgotten about, but can be just as funny, moving and interesting as longer writing. Writing short stories or poetry yourself can be a great way of experimenting with an idea to see if it works.

Challenge 1

Read the poem below and answer the questions that follow on a separate piece of paper.

'The Listeners' by Walter de la Mare

'Is there anybody there?' said the Traveller,
  Knocking on the moonlit door;
And his horse in the silence champed the grasses
  Of the forest's ferny floor:
And a bird flew up out of the turret,
  Above the Traveller's head:
And he smote upon the door again a second time;
  'Is there anybody there?' he said.
But no one descended to the Traveller;
  No head from the leaf-fringed sill
Leaned over and looked into his grey eyes,
  Where he stood perplexed and still.
But only a host of phantom listeners
  That dwelt in the lone house then
Stood listening in the quiet of the moonlight
  To that voice from the world of men:
Stood thronging the faint moonbeams on the dark stair,
  That goes down to the empty hall,

Hearkening in an air stirred and shaken
  By the lonely Traveller's call.
And he felt in his heart their strangeness,
  Their stillness answering his cry,
While his horse moved, cropping the dark turf,
  'Neath the starred and leafy sky;
For he suddenly smote on the door, even
  Louder, and lifted his head:—
'Tell them I came, and no one answered,
  That I kept my word,' he said.
Never the least stir made the listeners,
  Though every word he spake
Fell echoing through the shadowiness of the still house
  From the one man left awake:
Ay, they heard his foot upon the stirrup,
  And the sound of iron on stone,
And how the silence surged softly backward,
  When the plunging hoofs were gone.

a) The poem is called 'The Listeners'. Why do you think this is? (1)

b) We do not learn the Traveller's name in the poem. What effect does this create? Give evidence from the poem to support your answer. (3)

c) In your own words, how does the Traveller feel when no one answers his second knock? (2)

d) i) Who are the listeners that hear the Traveller? (2)

   ii) How does the Traveller respond to them? (3)

e) i) When the Traveller knocks for a third time, what does he say? (1)

   ii) What do we learn about his character from this? Support your answer with evidence from the passage. (3)

f) Identify two separate literary techniques used in the poem. What effects do they create? (6)

Score: _____ / 21

Think about three memorable characters in any books, stories or poems that you have read.

Draw three mind maps on a separate piece of paper to show what makes them memorable. Is it the dialogue? Is it their quirky personality? Are they likeable? Try to think of key moments in the literature that make the characters seem realistic and rounded.

Top Tip

Talking of someone's 'quirks' refers to the little unusual details of their personality.

Score: _____ / 3

Challenge 3

Create your own memorable character. Use the labelled boxes below to develop your ideas for a life-like figure.

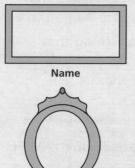

Name

Quirks

Physical attributes

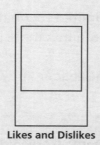

Likes and Dislikes

Possessions

Occupation

Top Tip

When answering comprehension questions about characters, think about how you *expect* them to behave. Sometimes a character might overturn your expectations. For example, in *Dr Jekyll and Mr Hyde*, the reputable Dr Jekyll leads a double life and at night transforms into the unscrupulous Mr Hyde.

Score: _____ / 6

Now Try This!

Read the extract below and answer the question that follows.

Rocky, you see, lived down on Long Island somewhere, miles away from New York; and not only that, but he had told me himself more than once that he never got up before twelve, and seldom earlier than one. Constitutionally the laziest young devil in America, he had hit on a walk in life which enabled him to go the limit in that direction. He was a poet. At least, he wrote poems when he did anything; but most of his time, as far as I could make out, he spent in a sort of trance. He told me once that he could sit on a fence, watching a worm and wondering what on earth it was up to, for hours at a stretch.
He had his scheme of life worked out to a fine point. About once a month he would take three days writing a few poems; the other three hundred and twenty-nine days of the year he rested.

From *The Aunt and the Sluggard*, by P G Wodehouse

Top Tip

This extract by P G Wodehouse creates an amusing image of Rocky. Look out for humour in comprehension texts and think about how the author has used language and sentence structure to make the piece witty. It's easy to forget that writing is often intended to entertain when doing a comprehension exercise!

How is Rocky presented in this extract?
A   Artistic and hardworking
B   A keen walker and traveller
C   Deeply religious
D   Creative and indolent
E   Ponderous and leisurely

Score: _____ / 1

Total score _____ / 31

LOW   CONFIDENCE   HIGH

Let's Get S-t-r-e-t-c-h-i-n-g!

Some questions will expect you to infer. This means that you will need to 'read between the lines' and deduce information about the story, rather than just answer fact-finding questions. When you do this, try to:

- think about what the author is saying in greater depth; don't just rely on the facts in front of you
- question how characters think and feel; just as in real life, we are sometimes sarcastic or say things we don't mean, and people in stories can do this too
- think about what is revealed can be limited to what the characters know, or the narrator can be omniscient (knowing everything that happens in stories)
- look out for dramatic irony (where the reader knows more than the characters).

Top Tip

The best way to become a skilled inferential reader is to read as widely – and as much – as possible. Choose books across a range of genres and time periods to help attune your eye to the different rhythms of various writers' voices.

Challenge 1

This extract is from the beginning of a novel. We are introduced to Mr Tulliver and his son, Tom.

"What I want, you know," said Mr Tulliver,—"what I want is to give Tom a good eddication; an eddication as'll be a bread to him. That was what I was thinking of when I gave notice for him to leave the academy at Lady-day. I mean to put him to a downright good school at Midsummer. The two years at th' academy 'ud ha' done well enough, if I'd meant to make a miller and farmer of him, for he's had a fine sight more schoolin' nor *I* ever got. All the learnin' *my* father ever paid for was a bit o' birch at one end and the alphabet at th' other. But I should like Tom to be a bit of a scholard, so as he might be up to the tricks o' these fellows as talk fine and write with a flourish. It 'ud be a help to me wi' these lawsuits, and arbitrations, and things. I wouldn't make a downright lawyer o' the lad,—I should be sorry for him to be a raskill,—but a sort o' engineer, or a surveyor, or an auctioneer and vallyer, like Riley, or one o' them smartish businesses as are all profits and no outlay, only for a big watch-chain and a high stool."

From *The Mill on the Floss*, by George Eliot

What can you infer about Mr Tulliver? How can you tell?

_____

_____

_____

_____

_____

Score: _____ /6

Read the extract below and answer the questions that follow on a separate piece of paper.

"I believe I can do it," she chuckled. The next moment she had climbed nimbly to the window ledge. From there it was an easy matter to step to the nearest tree-branch. Then, clinging like a monkey, she swung herself from limb to limb until the lowest branch was reached. The drop to the ground was – even for Pollyanna, who was used to climbing trees – a little fearsome. She took it, however, with bated breath, swinging from her strong little arms, and landing on all fours in the soft grass. Then she picked herself up and looked eagerly about her.

She was at the back of the house. Before her lay a garden in which a bent old man was working. Beyond the garden a little path through an open field led up a steep hill, at the top of which a lone pine tree stood on guard beside the huge rock. To Pollyanna, at the moment, there seemed to be just one place in the world worth being in – the top of that big rock.

From *Pollyanna*, by Eleanor H Porter

a) What do we learn of Pollyanna's character in the extract? Use your own words. (3)

b) What do you think will happen next? Support your answer with evidence from the passage. (3)

Score: _____ / 6

Challenge 3

Choose one of the opening lines below to begin a story of around 500 words which requires the reader to use inference to learn more about what is happening. Write your story on a separate sheet of paper.

The trees beyond the barn swayed as the wind whipped up the grass.
Against the harsh concrete of the city, dawn broke softly.
It was as if he had stepped back in time as he faced what was before him.
Bustling children streamed across the playground.

She took a deep breath and stepped forward.

Top Tip

In your own writing, you can experiment with your readers' ability to use inference. Writers are often told 'show, don't tell'. This means that it is more exciting to imply details about what is happening rather than making things too obvious for the reader.

Score: _____ / 15

Now Try This!

Read the extract below and answer the question that follows.

As he was sitting at breakfast next morning, Basil Hallward was shown into the room. "I am so glad I have found you, Dorian," he said gravely. "I called last night, and they told me you were at the opera. Of course, I knew that was impossible. But I wish you had left word where you had really gone to. I passed a dreadful evening, half afraid that one tragedy might be followed by another. I think you might have telegraphed for me when you heard of it first. I read of it quite by chance in a late edition of *The Globe* that I picked up at the club. I came here at once and was miserable at not finding you. I can't tell you how heart-broken I am about the whole thing. I know what you must suffer. But where were you?"

From *The Picture of Dorian Gray*, by Oscar Wilde

What do we learn about Dorian in the extract?
A He is an actor
B He is elusive and mysterious
C He makes others happy with his presence
D It is possible to read of his exploits in the paper
E He does not want to be discovered

Score: _____ / 1

Total score _____ / 28

LOW CONFIDENCE HIGH

Let's Get S-t-r-e-t-c-h-i-n-g!

The English language contains lots of words that follow a particular spelling rule, but there are lots of exceptions too. Two aspects of spelling that can cause confusion are:

- words with the vowel digraph 'ei' or 'ie'
- plural forms.

Top Tip

Reading extensively means you will come across a wide range of new vocabulary, which will help you in the 11+ test and beyond.

Challenge 1

Write the correct spelling for the answer to each given clue.
Each answer is a word with the 'ei' or 'ie' digraph.

a) Proof you have paid for something   ~~reicei~~ receipt ✓

b) The square root of sixty-four   eight ✓

c) Give way to something   yield ✓

d) Aggressive   fierce ✓

e) A pale brown colour   beige ✓

Score: 5 /5

Challenge 2

Write each word in the correct column in the table below.

protein glacier height eight believe ancient
forfeit deceit field science receipt

Words spelt ei after 'c' with an 'ee' sound	Words spelt ei with an 'ee', 'ay', 'ih' or an 'i' sound	Words spelt ie with an 'ee' sound	Exceptions
receipt ✓ deceit	protein forfeight ✓ height eight	field believe ✓	science ancient ~~dec~~ glacier ✓

Score: 11 /11

Challenge 3

Underline the correct plural of each singular word below.

oasis — **oases** / oasus

appendix — **appendices** / appendia

medium — mediae / **media**

axis — axia / **axes**

die — dices / **dice**

larva — **larvae** / larvia

Top Tip

Some words are the same in the plural as they are in the singular.

Score: 6 /6

Challenge 4

Write the plural form of each singular word.

a) goose _geese_ ✓

b) trout _trount_ ✓

c) diagnosis _diagnoses_ ✓

d) ellipsis _ellipses_ ✓

e) quiz _quizzes_ ✓

f) series _series_ ✓

g) leaf _leaves_ ✓

h) ox _oxen_ ✓

i) aircraft _aircraft_ ✓

Score: 9 /9

Now Try This!

On each numbered line there is either one spelling mistake or no mistake.
Write A, B, C or D to show where the mistake occurs. If there is no mistake, write N.

1. George, who lives in America, hopes to <u>recieve</u> a letter from his cousin Alex in England.
   A   B   (C)   D   ✓

2. I <u>shreiked</u> when I saw a huge, hairy spider crawling across my bedspread.
   (A)   B   C   D   ✓

3. During our hike in the countryside, we came across a herd of deers in the forest.
   A   B   C   (D)   ✓

4. Ravid has drawn a square-based pyramid which has four faces and five <u>vertixes</u>.
   A   B   C   (D)

Score: 4 /4

Total score 35 /35

LOW CONFIDENCE HIGH

English 41

Let's Get S-t-r-e-t-c-h-i-n-g!

Let's stretch your knowledge of prefixes and suffixes!
It's important to know which prefixes go with which words. Some prefixes have a negative or opposite meaning.
Sometimes the spelling of the root word changes when a suffix is added. Some suffixes, such as '-ance' and '-ence', and '-able' and '-ible', are tricky because they sound the same but have a different spelling.

Challenge 1

Add a prefix to each word below to form its antonym (opposite meaning).

a) **im**practical ✓

b) **mis**inform ✓

c) **in**definite ✓

d) **de**compose ✓

e) **un**even ✓

f) **ir**respective ✓

g) **dis**trust

h) **ill**legal ✓

i) **in**active

Top Tip
If the root word starts with 'm' or 'p', the prefix 'im' is used.

Top Tip
If the root word starts with 'l', the prefix 'il' is used. If the root word starts with 'r', the prefix 'ir' is generally used.

Score: __9__ /9

Challenge 2

What is the meaning of the emboldened prefixes in the words below?

a) **semi**-detached   **semi**-circle — half ✓

b) **mono**tone   **mono**rail — ~~f~~ one '½' Single ✓

c) **uni**versity   **uni**form — everybody ✓

d) **sub**way   **sub**ordinate — down / below

e) **auto**pilot   **auto**biography — self ✓

f) **super**man   **super**market — bigger ✓

g) **tele**vision   **tele**scope — far away ✓

h) **bi**cycle   **bi**centenary — two ✓

Score: __8__ /8

Challenge 3

a) Turn each noun into an adjective by adding the suffix '-cious' or '-tious'.

   i) malice ___malicious___ ✓   ii) repetition ___repetitious___ ✓

   iii) space ___~~sap~~ spacious___ ✓   iv) infect ___infectious___ ✓

Top Tip

If the root word ends in 'ce', the **suffix '-cious'** is usually used. If a related word ends in 'tion', the **suffix '-tious'** is usually used.

b) Turn each noun into an adjective by adding the suffix '-tial' or '-cial'.

   i) confidence ___confidential___   ii) essence ___essential___ .

   iii) face ___facial___ ✓   iv) president ___presidential___ ✓

Top Tip

The **suffix '-cial'** is usually used after a vowel and the **suffix '-tial'** is usually used after a consonant. But watch out for exceptions!

Score: __8__ /8

Challenge 4

a) Rewrite each verb as a noun by adding the suffix '-ance' or '-ence'.

   i) ally ___~~ally~~ alliance___   ii) differ ___difference___

   iii) insure ___insurance___   iv) tolerate ___~~toleterance~~___

   v) adhere ___adherence___   vi) obey ___obedience___

Top Tip

Where a verb ends in '-y', '-ure' or '-ear', the noun will usually take the suffix '-ance'. Where a verb ends in '-ere' or '-er', the noun will usually take the suffix '-ence'.

b) Add the suffixes '-ence', '-ed' and '-ing' to the verbs 'prefer' and 'infer'.

   i) prefer ___preference___   ___preferred___   ___preferring___ ✓

   ii) infer ___inference___   ___inferred___   ___inferring___ ✓

Top Tip

When a suffix beginning with a vowel is added to a word ending in '-fer', the 'r' is doubled if the 'fer' is still stressed when the suffix is added.

Score: __8__ /8

Now Try This!

On each numbered line there is either one spelling mistake or no mistake.
Write A, B, C or D to show where the mistake occurs. If there is no mistake, write N.

1. Our opponents scored the winning goal seconds before the referree blew the whistle.

   A _____ B _____ (C) _____ D

2. Oliver is great at offering inpartial advice during his sisters' frequent arguments.

   A _____ (B) _____ C _____ D

3. The ficticious rumour about the teacher's impending retirement has been quashed.

   (A) _____ B _____ C _____ D

4. With some degree of hesitency, Jack crept cautiously down the cellar steps.

   A _____ (B) _____ C _____ D

Score: __4__ /4

Total score _____ /37

LOW   CONFIDENCE   HIGH

English

Let's Get S-t-r-e-t-c-h-i-n-g!

Some words are tricky to spell for different reasons; it might be because they have a silent letter, an unpronounced syllable or because they have a foreign origin.

Homophones sound the same as another word but have a different meaning and spelling.

Near-homophones sound *almost* the same as another word but have a different meaning and spelling.

Challenge 1

There is a missing silent letter in each of the words below.

Write the correct spellings on the line beside each.

a) neumonia _____   b) silouette _____

c) sychology _____   d) rombus _____

e) doutful _____   f) veicle _____

g) terodactyl _____   h) nead _____

Score: _____ / 8

Challenge 2

Find the word in each sentence below that is missing its **silent letter**.

Rewrite the word correctly on the answer line.

a) The choir led the congregation in singing a solem hymn. _____

b) We took excellent photos of the famous parlament building. _____

c) The shopkeeper gave me a receit for my purchase. _____

d) Carla forged ahead, refusing to succum to the fear she felt. _____

e) The goverment held an emergency meeting to discuss the crisis. _____

Score: _____ / 5

Challenge 3

a) Circle the correct word in each **homophone** pair in bold in the sentences below.

   i) We watched the parade in celebration of the queen's 60-year **reign / rein**.

   ii) I decided to **alter / altar** the annoying ringtone on my new phone.

   iii) After the wild weather, the trees are almost completely **bare / bear**.

   iv) I noticed a degree of **dissent / descent** amongst the members at tonight's meeting.

   v) Dad helped me to **practice / practise** my lines for the school play.

b) Write a **near-homophone** for each word below.

   i) addition _____   ii) proceed _____   iii) accept _____

   iv) seize _____   v) access _____   vi) desert _____

Score: _____ / 11

Challenge 4

Find the 22 words that have been spelt incorrectly in the passage and write their correct spelling on the lines below. The words are a mixture of homophones, near-homophones and tricky words.

We couldn't go camping in the end dew to the bad whether sew we preceded to make alternitive plans. Their was a guessed house on the coast that we'd stayed in before witch we new was reasonibly prised with a grate view of the sea. We set off very early so we we're quiet wary when we finaly arrived. The seenery was spectaculer and we ventured down to the beech. They're were countless rockpools to explore but we prefered building damns in the sand.

_____

_____

_____

_____

Score: _____ / 11

Now Try This!

On each numbered line there is either one spelling mistake or no mistake.
Write A, B, C or D to show where the mistake occurs. If there is no mistake, write N.

1. From my window, I could see a mysterious shadow wondering around in the garden.
   A   B   C   D

2. Harry offered me some good advise about my interview which is scheduled tomorrow.
   A   B   C   D

3. The young couple applied for a licence so that they could marry in the autumn.
   A   B   C   D

Score: _____ / 3

Total score _____ / 38

LOW   CONFIDENCE   HIGH

Let's Get S-t-r-e-t-c-h-i-n-g!

Punctuation is used in writing to separate sentences, clauses, phrases and words. It helps to make the intended meaning of the writing clear. Punctuation also refers to the correct use of capital letters.

- **Capital letters** come at the start of sentences and proper nouns.
- **Commas** can be used to separate items in a list, after a fronted adverbial or fronted subordinate clause, or to avoid ambiguity; they can also demarcate words in parenthesis (see page 50).
- **Inverted commas** show the start and the end of direct speech. The final inverted commas come *after* the final punctuation mark, which might be a comma, a full stop, a question mark or an exclamation mark.

> **Top Tip**
>
> An **exclamation sentence** often starts with 'What...', or 'How...', contains a verb and ends with an exclamation mark.

Challenge 1

a) Rewrite each sentence using correct punctuation.

   i) how shocking the weather was on monday

   _____

   ii) neil armstrong was an american astronaut and the first man on the moon

   _____

b) Find the sentence that should **not** end with an exclamation mark.

   Watch out for broken glass ☐   How amazing your new hair cut is ☐

   What is the best novel you've ever read ☐   What a lovely view that is ☐

   Score: _____ / 3

Challenge 2

a) Insert the missing commas in the sentences below.

   i) If you turn right at the end of the road you'll see the church the car park and the cemetery on the left-hand side.

   ii) Before we ate Freda Malachy Klaus and Nav insisted on going for some fresh air.

b) How does a comma change the meaning of the second sentence below?

   Finlay asked if Stanley Morgan and Jamie would come to his house for a sleepover.
   Finlay asked if Stanley, Morgan and Jamie would come to his house for a sleepover.

   _____

   _____

   Score: _____ / 3

Insert the missing inverted commas in the direct speech below.

a) I'd give anything to be lying on a beach, sighed Maggie. I'm so fed up.

b) There's no point in moaning, said Archie, because you know Dad said we can't go this year.

c) Well, the last thing I want to do is go camping again, Archie. It'll be cold, wet and boring.

d) How do you know? Do you have a crystal ball? Archie demanded, crossly.

Score: _____ / 4

Challenge 4

Correct the punctuation in the passage below. Some is missing and some is incorrect. The first one has been done for you.

M
matthew has just read an article about dr thompson it seems that he likes a cup of hot

chocolate at bedtime a piece of toast and a biscuit one of his colleagues revealed: he is firm but

fair in the summer time he loves going camping with his wife and children he particularly likes

warwick castle malmesbury abbey and blenheim palace in the cotswolds

Score: _____ / 21

Now Try This!

On each numbered line of this passage there is either one punctuation mistake or no mistake. Write A, B, C or D to show where the mistake occurs. If there is no mistake, write N.

1. With a quick glance at his watch the marathon runner eased into the last mile. He sensed

   A   B   C   D

2. the competition creeping up behind him – even the briefest of looks would cost him

   A   B   C   D

3. precious time, time he couldn't afford to waste. "I've got this", he said to himself. Drawing

   A   B   C   D

4. on his last reserves of physical energy and mental determination he strove for the line.

   A   B   C   D

Score: _____ / 4

Total score _____ / 35

LOW   CONFIDENCE   HIGH

Let's Get S-t-r-e-t-c-h-i-n-g!

An apostrophe can be used to indicate a contraction or possession:

- A **contraction** is a shortened form of a word from which one or more letters have been omitted. The apostrophe is positioned exactly above where the missing letter, or letters, would be.
- To show **possession** in *singular* nouns, the apostrophe comes after the word followed by the letter 's'; to show possession in *plural* nouns, the apostrophe comes *after* the letter 's' that makes the noun plural; to show possession in *irregular plural* nouns, the apostrophe comes after the plural noun and *before* the letter 's'.

> **Top Tip**
>
> When a proper noun ends in the letter 's', the apostrophe is added followed by the letter 's'. However, you may also see an apostrophe with no letter 's'.
>
> For example:
> *Chris's shoes*
> *Chris' shoes*

Challenge 1

Tick one box in each row to show how the apostrophe is used in each sentence.

Sentence	Contraction	Possession
There've been lots of robberies in our local area recently.		
Celia's friends are coming round to celebrate her birthday.		
I could have sworn you're related to my next-door neighbour.		
You really will be shocked when you see Mum's new haircut.		

Score: _____ / 4

Challenge 2

a) Write the contracted forms of the following words.

i) should have _____

ii) they would _____

iii) shall not _____

iv) I had _____

v) will not _____

vi) could not have _____

b) Add an apostrophe to each phrase below.

i) the princes crown

ii) those princes crowns

iii) the foxs cubs

iv) the foxes dens

v) the childrens ski school

vi) the mens changing rooms

Score: _____ / 12

Challenge 3

Add an apostrophe to the word *its* where needed in the passage below.

Cautiously, the lion nudges i t s young cubs and pushes them along the savannah. I t s cooler now as the sun is starting to lose i t s intense heat as it starts i t s descent below the horizon. The youngest cub tries to catch up with i t s family but i t s hard to match their eager pace. Soon, they find themselves on the edge of the jungle; i t s a riot of noise but i t s not long before they find a quiet clearing in which to bed down for the night.

Score: _____ / 4

Challenge 4

Insert the missing apostrophes in the passage below.

The recent unpredictable weathers playing havoc with Dads vegetables. Hes been out there from the crack of dawn for weeks, digging and planting, though admittedly Mums helped him from time to time. Hes had the usual trouble with caterpillars and slugs as well, but even he wasnt expecting the extent to which theyve eaten through his cabbages and lettuces. Were normally tucking into home-grown tomatoes and cucumber at this time of year but it isnt looking like theyll be adorning our plates any time soon. Luckily, the local farmers vegetables have not been affected so I think well be paying them a visit.

Score: _____ / 12

Now Try This!

On each numbered line there is either one punctuation mistake or no mistake.
Write A, B, C or D to show where the mistake occurs. If there is no mistake, write N.

1. Amies hoping to visit her cousins in Nottingham next week if the train strike has ended by then.
   A   B   C   D

2. The committee members have agreed a budget of £3,000 to refurbish the womens changing rooms.
   A   B   C   D

3. When were in the car on long journeys, we either sing songs (badly, says Dad) or play 'I Spy'.
   A   B   C   D

Score: _____ / 3

Total score _____ / 35

LOW   CONFIDENCE   HIGH

Let's Get S-t-r-e-t-c-h-i-n-g!

Brackets can be used before and after a word, phrase or clause in parenthesis, either in the middle of a sentence or at the end.
Dashes and **commas** can also be used in parenthesis.
Single dashes can indicate additional information to a preceding clause. They can also be used for dramatic effect, to signal an interruption or a change in direction.
Colons can be used after a clause, to introduce another clause that explains or gives more detail about the first. A colon can also introduce a list or be used instead of a comma to introduce a quotation.
Semi-colons can be used instead of a full stop to link two closely related, independent clauses. Semi-colons can also be used to separate items in a list where the items themselves contain commas, helping to avoid confusion.

Top Tip

The words in parenthesis might be a relative clause, a prepositional phrase, a noun phrase, an adverbial phrase, a subordinate clause, a main clause or even a single word.

Challenge 1

Insert either a single dash or double dashes in each sentence below.

a) My mum is a famous author and poet you'll definitely have heard of her.

b) Without a doubt, Millie's resilience not to mention her extreme courage saw her through the awful ordeal.

c) Our trek through the Amazon rainforest incredible as it was left me feeling weak and exhausted.

Score: _____ /3

Challenge 2

Rewrite each sentence below with the punctuation marks in the correct position.

a) This week we are covering the following: in maths area, perimeter and volume.

_____

b) Erin's been visiting Scotland for years she loves the scenery; and the people.

_____

c) The judge in the murder trial announced – his verdict guilty.

_____

Score: _____ /3

Challenge 3

a) Insert a colon and three semi-colons in the sentence below.

I'd really love to visit the following places the wild national parks on the island of Hokkaido, Japan the Grotta Azzurra on the island of Capri, Italy Recoleta and La Boca, Buenos Aires and the Niagara Falls in Ontario, Canada.

b) Insert a pair of dashes, a colon, a pair of brackets and a single dash in the short passage below.

After the performance, Mr McGrath our drama teacher made his final announcement "Please take care as the car park will be busy." We all filed outside it was dark already and searched for our parents' cars. It had been a great show an experience I'll never forget.

Score: _____ / 8

Challenge 4

Insert the missing punctuation around the words in parenthesis in each sentence.

a) The surgeon with her usual dexterity performed the life-saving operation to the relief of all.

b) We'd intended to take the early train the show was a matinee but unfortunately it was cancelled.

c) Our school caretaker who's an avid reader and researcher is appearing on *Mastermind* this week.

d) Gustav and Mo admired but didn't buy the painting that was on display.

Top Tip

When you take the word or words that are in parenthesis out of the sentence, what is left still makes sense – it is a main clause.

Score: _____ / 4

Now Try This!

On each numbered line of this passage there is either one punctuation mistake or no mistake. Write A, B, C or D to show where the mistake occurs. If there is no mistake, write N.

1. On the island were a rainforest, fresh water and exotic fruits everything the explorers had hoped

    A   B   C   D

2. for. Hugo always the first to do anything – made a beeline for the coconuts which had fallen

    A   B   C   D

3. generously from the palm trees. Helen ran to the pool at the bottom of the waterfall carefully, she

    A   B   C   D

4. leaned over the edge and filled her flask with the cool water. It was then that she heard the growl.

    A   B   C   D

Score: _____ / 4

Total score _____ / 22

LOW   CONFIDENCE   HIGH

English   51

Let's Get S-t-r-e-t-c-h-i-n-g!

Grammar is the system of rules used in speaking and writing.
Test questions could challenge your knowledge of:

- consistency of verb tenses within a sentence or passage
- subject-verb agreement
- formal and informal versions of English (i.e. Standard and non-Standard English)
- the subjunctive mood, which is often used when expressing a wish, an emotion, a possibility, or an action that has not yet occurred. For example: *It is essential that you be careful when taking the cliff path.*

> **Top Tip**
> The subject in a sentence is the person, animal or thing that is carrying out the action, shown by the verb. The verb tells you what the subject is 'doing', 'being' or 'having'.

Challenge 1

a) Underline the verbs in the passage below. **(18)**

A few years ago, we decide to go camping. It was our first time and I must say, we were very excited. Little do we know that it is going to rain the entire time! However, I wouldn't say it ruins our trip – we are able to spend the evenings in the recreation room where we play table tennis and meet lots of new friends.

b) Now rewrite the passage, correcting any verbs that are in the wrong tense. **(7)**

_____

_____

_____

_____

_____

_____

Score: _____ /25

Challenge 2

> **Top Tip**
> In Standard English, the correct grammar is used.

Rewrite each sentence below in Standard English.

a) We seen them same street musicians when we went shopping last week.

_____

b) Salena said she would of took her little brother to the park if she'd been asked.

Score: _____ /2

Challenge 3

Underline the subject in each sentence below.

a) Looking around him, Rick was certain he'd been here before.

b) "Please will you call an electrician?"

c) The amazing acrobats thrilled us with their breathtaking acts.

d) Buckingham Palace is one of London's most popular tourist attractions.

Top Tip

The subject can be a noun, a proper noun, a pronoun or a noun phrase.

Score: _____ / 4

Challenge 4

Insert the correct form of the verb *to be* to complete each sentence.

a) A group of Year 6 children _____ representing the school at the environmental debate.

b) Mum said my sister and I _____ allowed to go into town on our new bikes.

c) If I _____ to win a million pounds, I'd cruise around the Caribbean.

d) Should you _____ cold, please turn on the heating.

Top Tip

You will often find the subjunctive mood in formal speech and writing.

Score: _____ / 4

Now Try This!

Choose the correct option, A, B, C, D or E, to complete each numbered line of this passage.

1. As I recalled

this	them	those	that	there
A	B	C	D	E

long-

2. ago school days, my eyes

full up	are filling up	filling up	fill up	filled up
A	B	C	D	E

3. with tears. How happy we

are being	was	have been	had been	were being
A	B	C	D	E

4. back then

as	whereas	although	since	with
A	B	C	D	E

young children!

Score: _____ / 4

Total score _____ / 39

LOW   CONFIDENCE   HIGH

English   53

Read this passage carefully, then answer questions 1–15.

The Doll's House

by Katherine Mansfield

> *In the story, Kezia, Isabel and Lottie have received a present from Mrs Hay.*

1 When dear old Mrs. Hay went back to town after staying with the Burnells she sent the children a doll's house. It was so big that the carter and Pat carried it into the courtyard, and there it stayed, propped up on two wooden boxes beside the feed-room door. No harm could come to it; it was summer. And perhaps the smell of paint would have gone off by the time it had to be taken in.

5 For, really, the smell of paint coming from that doll's house ("Sweet of old Mrs. Hay, of course; most sweet and generous!") — but the smell of paint was quite enough to make anyone seriously ill, in Aunt Beryl's opinion. Even before the sacking was taken off. And when it was. . . .

There stood the doll's house, a dark, oily, spinach green, picked out with bright yellow. Its two solid little chimneys, glued on to the roof, were painted red and white, and the door, gleaming with 10 yellow varnish, was like a little slab of toffee. Four windows, real windows, were divided into panes by a broad streak of green. There was actually a tiny porch, too, painted yellow, with big lumps of congealed paint hanging along the edge.

But perfect, perfect little house! Who could possibly mind the smell? It was part of the joy, part of the newness.

15 "Open it quickly, someone!"

The hook at the side was stuck fast. Pat pried it open with his penknife, and the whole house front swung back, and—there you were, gazing at one and the same moment into the drawing-room and dining-room, the kitchen and two bedrooms. That is the way for a house to open! Why don't all houses open like that? How much more exciting than peering through the slit of a door into 20 a mean little hall with a hatstand and two umbrellas! That is—isn't it?—what you long to know about a house when you put your hand on the knocker. Perhaps it is the way God opens houses at the dead of night when He is taking a quiet turn with an angel. . . .

"O-oh!" The Burnell children sounded as though they were in despair. It was too marvellous; it was too much for them. They had never seen anything like it in their lives. All the rooms were 25 papered. There were pictures on the walls, painted on the paper, with gold frames complete. Red carpet covered all the floors except the kitchen; red plush chairs in the drawing-room, green in the dining-room; tables, beds with real bedclothes, a cradle, a stove, a dresser with tiny plates and one big jug. But what Kezia liked more than anything, what she liked frightfully, was the lamp. It stood in the middle of the dining-room table, an exquisite little amber lamp with a white globe. It was 30 even filled all ready for lighting, though, of course, you couldn't light it. But there was something inside that looked like oil and moved when you shook it.

The father and mother dolls, who sprawled very stiff as though they had fainted in the drawing-room, and their two little children asleep upstairs, were really too big for the doll's house. They didn't look as though they belonged. But the lamp was perfect. It seemed to smile at Kezia, to say,
35 "I live here." The lamp was real.

The Burnell children could hardly walk to school fast enough the next morning. They burned to tell everybody, to describe, to—well—to boast about their doll's house before the school-bell rang.

"I'm to tell," said Isabel, "because I'm the eldest. And you two can join in after. But I'm to tell first."

There was nothing to answer. Isabel was bossy, but she was always right, and Lottie and Kezia
40 knew too well the powers that went with being eldest. They brushed through the thick buttercups at the road edge and said nothing.

"And I'm to choose who's to come and see it first. Mother said I might."

For it had been arranged that while the doll's house stood in the courtyard they might ask the girls at school, two at a time, to come and look. Not to stay to tea, of course, or to come traipsing
45 through the house. But just to stand quietly in the courtyard while Isabel pointed out the beauties, and Lottie and Kezia looked pleased. . . .

But hurry as they might, by the time they had reached the tarred palings of the boys' play-ground the bell had begun to jangle. They only just had time to whip off their hats and fall into line before the roll was called. Never mind. Isabel tried to make up for it by looking very important and
50 mysterious and by whispering behind her hand to the girls near her, "Got something to tell you at playtime."

Playtime came and Isabel was surrounded. The girls of her class nearly fought to put their arms round her, to walk away with her, to beam flatteringly, to be her special friend. She held quite a court under the huge pine trees at the side of the playground. Nudging, giggling together, the
55 little girls pressed up close. And the only two who stayed outside the ring were the two who were always outside, the little Kelveys. They knew better than to come anywhere near the Burnells.

Choose the best answer to each question. Look back at the passage if you need to.

1. What is the effect of the author writing 'dear old Mrs Hay' in line 1?　　　　　　　　　(1)

    A   It shows Mrs Hay wanted to give the children a present after she had been staying with the Burnell family.

    B   It exaggerates Mrs Hay's advanced age and suggests that she has forgotten what the Burnell children's behaviour is really like.

    C   It means the story opens with an atmosphere of kindness, in contrast to the Burnells' opinions towards other children.

    D   It means the story opens with an atmosphere of kindness, just like the Burnells' opinions towards other children.

    E   It shows the children were deserving of the present sent by Mrs Hay.

2. What atmosphere is created in paragraph 2 in the description of the doll's house? **(1)**

   A It creates an inviting, exciting atmosphere because the house seems deeply unappealing due to its imperfections.
   B It creates an air of disappointment because the paintwork is imperfect and the house is an unpleasant colour.
   C It creates an ominous atmosphere because the children are reluctant to open the doll's house.
   D It creates a confusing atmosphere because the sentences are long and the description of the doll's house is just a list of what can be seen from the outside.
   E It creates an inviting, exciting atmosphere because the house seems appealing even though it is not perfectly finished.

3. Look at the paragraph beginning on line 16 ('The hook at the side was stuck fast…')

   Why does the author structure the paragraph in this way? **(1)**

   A This creates a sense of excitement as the description mimics the reader seeing the house just as the children see it.
   B The initial description of the door being stuck makes the house seem old and unimpressive.
   C The use of rhetorical question makes it seem as though the narrator does not understand the doll's house very well.
   D The description of the hall makes the house seem like a disappointing present.
   E The description of the rooms is compared to peering through the door of the doll's house.

4. Which of the following are mentioned in the description of the doll's house? **(1)**

   i   A working lamp
   ii   Red chairs in the dining room
   iii Miniature crockery
   iv   There were five rooms in total
   v   Yellow detail on the porch

   A i, iii and iv   B All of the above   C i, iv and v   D iii, iv and v   E ii, iii and v

5. Why would the other children not be invited to stay to tea when they looked at the doll's house? **(1)**

   A Isabel does not enjoy having friends over very much.
   B When the children had previously come to play, they were clumsy with Isabel's toys.
   C The other children are considered inferior to the Burnell family.
   D The other children have to eat with Lottie and Kezia.
   E They might behave badly and show poor manners.

6. Why did Isabel tell the other girls she had news to share at playtime? **(1)**

   A To create suspense for the girls and dramatise the story she would be telling
   B To let them know she needed to talk to them at playtime
   C To make up for the girls being late to school
   D To ensure the other girls would try to walk with her
   E To show that the Burnell family are important in the village

7. 'She held quite a court under the huge pine trees' (lines 53–54). What does this mean?   (1)

    A   Isabel was on the outskirts of the group.
    B   Isabel was adeptly playing tennis.
    C   Isabel set up a game under the trees.
    D   Isabel was the centre of attention.
    E   Isabel was shaded by the trees.

8. Why did the Kelvey girls not come near Isabel in the playground?   (1)

    A   They couldn't squeeze near her as Isabel was surrounded.
    B   Isabel's friends did not approve of the Kelvey girls approaching her.
    C   The Kelveys were much younger than the other girls in the circle.
    D   The Kelvey girls were sworn enemies of the Burnells.
    E   It is implied that they are considered socially inferior to the other pupils.

9. 'Perhaps it is the way God opens houses at the dead of night when He is taking a quiet turn with an angel. . . .' (lines 21–22). What technique has the author used here?   (1)

    A   repetition   B   personification   C   simile   D   metaphor   E   hyperbole

10. Which of the following words is closest in meaning to the word 'palings' (line 47)?   (1)

    A   road   B   outskirts   C   fenceposts   D   playground   E   surfaces

11. 'It seemed to smile at Kezia, to say, "I live here."' What technique has the author used here?   (1)

    A   metaphor   B   simile   C   personification   D   hyperbole   E   enjambement

12. What does the word 'fall' mean in line 48?   (1)

    A   stumble   B   drop   C   arrive   D   decrease   E   assemble

13. 'Even before the sacking was taken off.' What part of speech is 'before'?   (1)

    A   pronoun   B   determiner   C   adverb   D   adjective   E   conjunction

14. 'The smell of paint coming from that doll's house.' What part of speech is 'that'?   (1)

    A   adjective   B   adverb   C   determiner   D   pronoun   E   preposition

15. 'It was too marvellous.' What part of speech is 'it'?   (1)

    A   adverb   B   adjective   C   preposition   D   pronoun   E   determiner

Questions 16–23 test spelling, grammar and punctuation.

16. Write the plural form of each noun below.   (6)

    a) analysis   _____   b) tuna   _____

    c) datum   _____   d) swine   _____

    e) series   _____   f) crisis _____

17. Rewrite the passage below with correct punctuation.   (3)

    its time to walk to the train station said frances we dont want to miss the 7:05

    isnt there a later train we can get asked doug if were there too early well only be hanging around

    better safe than sorry replied dougs sister emilie its too important we cant afford to be late

    _____

    _____

    _____

    _____

    _____

18. Rewrite each sentence using the correct form of the verbs.   (3)

    a) Charlie and Philippa has gone on holiday but they came back tomorrow.

    _____

    b) Before we are starting our test, our teacher is telling us to check each answer carefully.

    _____

    c) "When was you going to tell me that you couldn't be able to come to my party?"

    _____

19. Add a prefix to each word below to form its antonym (opposite meaning).   (4)

    a) _____active   b) _____literate

    c) _____penetrable   d) _____respect

20. Add a suitable suffix to each verb below to form a noun and adjective. (6)

reside   prefer   vacate   apply   consider   rely

Nouns	Adjectives

21. Find three incorrectly spelt words in each sentence. Write the correct spellings on the lines. (4)

a) No-one could beleive that the cheif of police was involved in such a decietful affair.

....

b) Chen speaks the French langage with amazing fluancy although strangly he's never set foot in France.

....

c) The casheir packed my caffiene-free tea and coffee then handed me my reciept.

....

d) The presidencial candidate was not aloud to leave without a significant amount of security.

....

22. Turn these nouns into adjectives by adding an appropriate suffix. (6)

a) space ....   b) fiction ....

c) benefit ....   d) repetition ....

e) malice ....   f) palace ....

23. Write the answer for each given clue. (3)

a) Comes after eleventh and before thirteenth ....

b) The noun formed from the verb 'obey' ....

c) The verb formed from the adjective 'intense' ....

Total score _____ / 50

LOW   CONFIDENCE   HIGH

Let's Get S-t-r-e-t-c-h-i-n-g!

You need to be prepared to:
- find four-letter words hidden across the end of one word and the start of the next word
- identify how the first word of a pair has been changed to create the second word, and apply this change to a new pair of words.

Challenge 1

a) Find **three** four-letter words in each word below. The letters are in consecutive order.

fundamentalist   ....

restaurant   ....

motherboard   ....

b) Find **four** four-letter words you can make from the word 'hidden'. The letters can be used in any order.

....

Score: _____ / 4

Challenge 2

What is the rule for creating the second word from the first word in each of these pairs?

a) (wrapper   pea)   (slatted   tea)

_____

b) (moth   them)   (post   step)

_____

c) (flower   wolf)   (stared   rats)

_____

> **Problem Solving**
> Check for letters that have been removed or added in each word pair.

> **Top Tip**
> Look out for words that have been reversed!

Score: _____ / 3

Challenge 3

Find **two** four-letter words 'hidden' across the gap in each sentence below. Each word is made from the end of one word and the beginning of the next.

a) With practice, James had the potential to be a great singer.

....

b) Use of lead-based paints proved the cause of the artist's death.

....

c) A musical medley comprising a range of acts received great reviews.

....

d) The lock needs to be fixed by a locksmith this instance.

....

Score: _____ / 8

Challenge 4

A four-letter word is 'hidden' across the gap in each sentence below, but the letters are in **reverse order**. Find the word in each sentence.

a) My cat captured a rodent in the back garden.

....

b) Harry exceeds in everything he ever does!

....

c) Last night, we had our piano rehearsal.

....

d) The vet said she must operate on Monty immediately.

....

Score: _____ / 4

Now Try This!

1. Underline the four-letter word hidden across the end of one word and the start of the next.
   a) It was breaktime but our teacher insisted we tidy up first.
   b) Another downside to my trip, apart from the weather, was the awful altitude sickness.

2. Find the word that completes the last pair of words in the same way as the other two pairs.
   a) (skating   sing)   (leopard   lard)   (biggest   [.................])
   b) (fairly   rail)   (salver   vale)   (wonder   [.................])

Score: _____ / 4

Total score _____ / 23

CONFIDENCE   LOW   HIGH

Let's Get S-t-r-e-t-c-h-i-n-g!

You need to be ready for questions that involve:

- completing a longer word that has three letters missing (which themselves form a word)
- working out how the letters in two words have been used to create a third word and then applying this rule to a new set of words.

Challenge 1

Find **three** three-letter words in each word below without changing the order of the letters.

a) searched ....

b) candidate ....

c) formidable ....

d) carpentry ....

e) brotherhood ....

Can you find **five** three-letter words in the following word?

f) psychotherapist ....

....

Score: _____ / 6

Challenge 2

Choose a three-letter word from the box to complete each word.

LAP	FUN	SPA	HIM	RIM	GOT	ICE	WON

a) _____ DERED

b) NEW_____ PER

c) C_____ INAL

d) _____ CTIONAL

e) L_____ NCE

f) NE_____ IATE

g) C_____ NEY

h) S_____ STICK

Score: _____ / 8

Challenge 3

In the first set of words on the left, the word in brackets has been formed from the letters of the two outer words. In the second set, which word in bold is created using the same rule as that in the first set?

Problem Solving

You can assign numbers (e.g. 1, 2, 3, 4 and 5, 6, 7, 8) to the two outside words in the first set. Then match the letters of the word in square brackets to these numbers. Apply this code to the second group of words and apply the number code from the middle word of the first set to the middle word of the second set.

a) bare [area] bear   beer [**rear rare bear**] aura

b) ratio [tore] quest   abide [**leaf full fall**] awful

c) foal [felt] teal   meal [**mash sham lash**] hams

Score: _____ / 3

Challenge 4

Find the word that has been spelt incorrectly in each sentence. The error occurs in a group of letters that themselves form a three-letter word. Write that three-letter word and then write another three-letter word that would correct the spelling.

a) We were very greatful for the donation to our chosen charity.

b) Our school's fandamental principle is to be successful.

c) I was surprised at the announcement that I'd won the compitition.

d) The mourners congregated calmly in the village cematery.

Score: _____ / 4

Now Try This!

1. Find the missing three-letter word to complete the words in capital letters.

Top Tip

Consider the context of the sentence to help you work out what the fully complete word ought to be.

a) Ester showed no enthusiasm or COMMITT to the project.

_____

b) In a moment of DESATION, Max flung himself on the bed and screamed.

_____

2. Work out the rule in the first set of words to find the missing word in the second set.

a) (cart [rat] tell)   (palm [_____] debt)

b) (theme [germ] cargo)   (blink [_____] whisk)

c) (lake [beak] able)   (brew [_____] area)

Score: _____ / 5

Total score _____ / 26

LOW   CONFIDENCE   HIGH

Working with Words 3

Let's Get S-t-r-e-t-c-h-i-n-g!

You need to be ready for questions that ask you to:

- move a letter from one word and add it to a second word to create two new words
- identify a word that can be linked (by its meaning) to two pairs of other words.

Challenge 1

Remove a letter from each given word on the right to find the answer to the clues on the left. Your words will form a jumbled sentence. Write the sentence correctly on the line below.

Young males	BUOYS
A female pronoun	SHED
Shown when very cross	DANGER
A preposition	BAT
Looked long and hard	STARRED
Another word for 'foolish'	SWILLY
A determiner	THEM
A preposition	BIN

Score: _____ /2

Challenge 2

Move one letter from the first word in each pair and add it to the second word to make two new words. The seven letters that you move can be rearranged to make a seven-letter word. Find the seven-letter word.

Problem Solving

Don't change the order of the other letters in the words.

Word pairs	New word pairs	Letter you moved
stand sable		
trend tough		
chart hump		
hone sank		
cream wan		
slope port		
twine lean		

Top Tip

Cover each letter of the first word one-by-one until you find a new word.

The seven-letter word is _____.

Score: _____ /8

a) Underline the **two** definitions in each box that **do not** have a connection to the word on the left.

i) press

smooth	persuade
button	iron
ask	sew
newspapers	journalists

ii) stand

vertical	sports ground structure
chill	act of opposition
opinion	able to bear something
care	stall

b) Write a homophone for each of these words.

i) aisle _____   ii) pear _____

iii) key _____   iv) birth _____

Score: _____ / 6

Add **one letter** to each word below to make a new word.
Write the new word on the line next to each.

a) debt _____   b) secret _____   c) griped _____

d) fright _____   e) tread _____   f) solder _____

Score: _____ / 6

1. Which letter can be moved from the first word to the second word to make two new words?

a) TROLL   COMPLAIN   _____

b) SAVIOUR   PANT   _____

c) ROUTE   BOY   _____

2. Which one of the five options goes equally well with both pairs of words in the brackets?

Problem Solving

Identify words that might belong to more than one word class, e.g. 'split' which can be a noun or a verb.

a) (fur skin)   (throw fling)

   A jacket   **B** pelt   **C** chuck   **D** hair   **E** layer

b) (light slight)   (swoon dizzy)

   A opaque   **B** feint   **C** feverish   **D** faint   **E** weak

Score: _____ / 5

Total score _____ / 27

LOW   CONFIDENCE   HIGH

VR   65

Let's Get S-t-r-e-t-c-h-i-n-g!

You will be tested on the meanings of words. Be prepared to identify:

- a pair of antonyms (words that are opposite in meaning)
- a pair of synonyms (words that are the same or similar in meaning)
- connections between the meanings of words.

Top Tip

Using a thesaurus in your writing will help you to expand your range of synonyms.

Challenge 1

Find **two** different meanings for each word below. Write **N** for **noun** or **V** for **verb** depending on the word class you have chosen.

Problem Solving

Remember that many words have more than one meaning.

bark

address

stem

Score: _____ /6

Challenge 2

Put each word below into the correct column according to its word class.

blow   devastate   glare   desk   itemise   breathe   level   candle   reporter

Verb	Noun	Can be both a verb and a noun

Score: _____ /9

a) Underline the **two words** in the sentence that are antonyms.

   As the troops *approached* the besieged city, the panicked inhabitants *retreated* into their homes.

Problem Solving

Remember to check that the words you identify as antonyms belong to the same word class. The same applies to synonyms.

b) Underline the **two words** in the sentence that are synonyms.

   The silversmith expertly fashioned a *delicate* flower pendant, each with exceptionally *fragile* petals.

c) Underline the **two words**, one from each set of brackets, that are most opposite in meaning.

   (dissent   altercation   subordination)   (discord   acceptance   refusal)

   (attraction   fascination   adoration)   (disinterest   disappointment   boredom)

   (whisper   secrete   divulge)   (sigh   misplace   expose)

   Score: _____ /5

Create **four** different word connection sentences using one word from each box in each sentence.

| fragile
seed
resolute
noun | is to | sow
determined
adjective
robust | as | timid
verb
faint
bulb | is to | plant
fainthearted
strong
adverb |

_____ is to _____ as _____ is to _____

_____ is to _____ as _____ is to _____

_____ is to _____ as _____ is to _____

_____ is to _____ as _____ is to _____

   Score: _____ /4

1. Underline **two words**, one from each set, that are most opposite in meaning.
   (resilient   different   cautious)   (desperate   vulnerable   careful)

2. Underline **two words**, one from each set, that are closest in meaning.
   (push   flog   snap)   (crash   thrash   buy)

3. Underline **two words**, one from each bracketed set, that will complete the sentence.
   sought is to (ought, should, seek) as **caught** is to (catch, throw, ball)

   Score: _____ /3

Total score _____ /27

LOW   CONFIDENCE   HIGH

VR   67

Let's Get S-t-r-e-t-c-h-i-n-g!

The wider your range of vocabulary, the better. Test questions could also ask you to:

- work out which two words can be joined to make a compound word
- identify two words that have a different meaning to the other three in a set of five words.

Top Tip

Reading a wide range of fiction and non-fiction will help you to expand your vocabulary base.

Challenge 1

Eight compound words have been mixed up below. The first part of each compound word has the wrong second part joined to it. Rearrange the words to form eight correct compound words.

crossdown   _____

deadpart   _____

threadpoint   _____

brainbeat   _____

comeover   _____

counterline   _____

pinbare   _____

downwash   _____

Score: _____ / 8

Challenge 2

Circle the word that is the odd one out in each set below.

a) love	anger	greed	fear	hate
b) calmly	softly	quickly	lovely	quietly
c) whale	platypus	dolphin	vole	chameleon
d) ludicrous	ridiculous	foolish	farcical	hilarious
e) prospect	view	landscape	scene	apparition
f) shoulder	knee	ear	knuckle	ankle

Score: _____ / 6

Challenge 3

Add another word to each given word to form a compound word.

a) mind.. b) check..

c) proof.. d) land..

Challenge 4

Underline the **two words** in each group that are most closely related in meaning.

a) tornado   autumn   gale   hail   hurricane

b) cauliflower   tomato   carrot   apple   potato

c) ship   transporter   cruiser   freighter   ferry

d) comet   sky   Earth   asteroid   summer

e) saunter   drop   dash   mark   fall

f) escalate   lower   raise   top   above

Problem Solving

Watch out for words with more than one meaning.

Now Try This!

1. Underline **two words**, one from each set, that combine to make a compound word.

   a) (letter water foot)   (tap stamp age)

   b) (yellow black green)   (list note sign)

2. Three of the following five words are related in some way.
   Underline the **two words** that are not related to the others.

   a) (doctor   nurse   hospital   surgeon   clinic)

   b) (parallelogram cuboid   quadrilateral cylinder   pentagon)

   c) (see   blurred   unclear   observe   obscured)

   d) (type   kind   genre   pleasant   fine)

   e) (aim   strike   goal   attack   purpose)

Total score _____ / 31

LOW   CONFIDENCE   HIGH

VR   69

Let's Get S-t-r-e-t-c-h-i-n-g!

You should be prepared to:

• find a letter to complete a pair of words

• identify what links one pair of letters to another pair of letters so that you can apply the same change to a new set of letters.

Use the alphabet to help you with the following challenges.

A B C D E F G H I J K L M N O P Q R S T U V W X Y Z

Challenge 1

In each pair below, the **same last letter** is needed to complete the two words. Find the letter.

a) ear   cul   ☐   b) sic   ban   ☐

c) clas   gri   ☐   d) kin   rac   ☐

e) stun   close   ☐   f) tall   spin   ☐

g) suit   met   ☐   h) ran   tin   ☐

i) van   rid   ☐   j) weir   bear   ☐

Score: _____ /10

Challenge 2

In each pair below, the **same first letter** is needed to complete the two words. Find the letter.

a) hack   rap   ☐   b) trip   care   ☐

c) late   tack   ☐   d) hen   elder   ☐

e) pirit   tride   ☐   f) lunk   rail   ☐

g) rave   ravel   ☐   h) awl   rawn   ☐

i) rope   rain   ☐   j) lame   eige   ☐

Problem Solving

If an answer isn't obvious to you, quickly work through the alphabet to help you find a letter that might fit.

Score: _____ /10

Insert the **same** letter to complete the first word and start the next.

a) gras_____ _____ulse

b) bul_____ _____rooch

c) sil_____ _____hreat

d) flan_____ _____nack

Challenge 4

a) Starting from the letter **A**, follow the instructions to make a four-letter word.

- Count forwards 3

- Count forwards 4

- Count forwards 1

- Count backwards 7

The word is _____

Top Tip

Visualise the alphabet as a circle to help you move from A to Z when counting forwards or from Z to A when counting backwards.

b) What is the rule for going from the first pair of letters to the second pair?

i) PM   VG   _____

ii) PQ   KO   _____

Now Try This!

1. Find the letter pair that completes each sentence.

a) **XD** is to **BZ** as **CR** is to **[?]**

   A GV   B FM   C BQ   D GN   E DE

b) **AZ** is to **BY** as **GT** is to **[?]**

   A SH   B FS   C FU   D HU   E HS

2. Find the letter that completes the first word and starts the second word in each pair.

a) plea [_____] arnish   ven [_____] raipse

b) lus [_____] andle   mulc [_____] oarse

Total score _____ /31

LOW   CONFIDENCE   HIGH

Let's Get S-t-r-e-t-c-h-i-n-g!

To solve some questions, you will need to find connections between a letter code and a word, or between a number code and a word.

Use the alphabet to help you with the following challenges.

A B C D E F G H I J K L M N O P Q R S T U V W X Y Z

Challenge 1

Find the word made from each set of instructions.

a) Starting from the letter **M**:

- count backwards 6 ☐

- count forwards 5 ☐

- count forwards 2 ☐

- count forwards 8 ☐

- count forwards 3 ☐

What word do the letters make?

_____

b) Starting from the letter **D**:

- count forwards 8 ☐

- count forwards 5 ☐

- count backwards 10 ☐

- count forwards 4 ☐

- count forwards 1 ☐

What word do the letters make?

_____

Score: _____ /2

Challenge 2

The number codes for three of these four words are given below.

MAID	NAME	LAND	LANE
2314	1357	6324	

If M = 1 and D = 7, work out the codes for the following letters:

a) A = _____   N = _____   E = _____   I = _____   L = _____

b) Write the code for the word **LANDMINE**.   _____

Problem Solving

Look for clues in the letters to help you work out the number codes quickly. For example, two words which have the same two letters in the middle will also have the same two numbers at the middle of their codes.

Score: _____ /2

Challenge 3

Crack the code! Use the following instructions to work out what the code below says:
- For each vowel, count forwards 3 letters in the alphabet.
- For each consonant, count backwards 3 letters in the alphabet.

DOH BRX D FRAH FODFNHO?

_____

Score: _____ / 5

Challenge 4

Sherlock Holmes is trying to crack a case. He's found a coded message that he hopes will lead him to a notorious jewel thief. His assistant, Dr Watson, has decoded the first two words.

Decode the rest of the message.

WVZI SLONVH,   **3IW QZMFZIB**

DEAR HOLMES,   _____

HLIIB R NRHHVW BLF! OLERMT GSV QVDVOH.

_____

GSV YOZXP KZMGSVI CC

_____

K.H. XZGXS NV RU BLF XZM!

_____

Score: _____ / 4

Now Try This!

1. If the code for **SNOW** is **TPRA**, what is **GNDOJ** the code for? _____

2. If the code for **DARK** is **XGLQ**, what is the code for **LIGHT**? _____

3. Three of these words have been given a number code.

   PEAT   LEAP   HELP   TALE

       1532   4236   6251

   Problem Solving

   If you are *given* the code, you need to *reverse* the pattern to find the word.

   a) Find the code for the word **HEAP**. _____

   b) Find the word that has the number code **6532**. _____

Score: _____ / 4

Total score _____ / 17

LOW   CONFIDENCE   HIGH

Let's Get S-t-r-e-t-c-h-i-n-g!

You may have to answer questions that test your skills working with sequences:

- You may have to work out the pattern between pairs of letters in a sequence and use the rule to find the next pair of letters in the series.
- You may have to work out the mathematical rule to find the next number in a sequence.

Use the alphabet to help you with the following challenges.

A B C D E F G H I J K L M N O P Q R S T U V W X Y Z

Challenge 1

Top Tip

You may have to count forwards or backwards to find the rule.

Imagine that there is a mirror line between the letters **M** and **N** in the alphabet. Decide whether to go left or right from the mirror line to find the two letters that complete each word.

a) SA_UR_TE   (7 letters from the mirror line; 13 letters from the mirror line)

b) M_THOLOG_CAL   (12 letters from the mirror line; 5 letters from the mirror line)

c) INF_ _IATE   (8 letters from the mirror line; 5 letters from the mirror line)

d) P_O_URE   (5 letters from the mirror line; 11 letters from the mirror line)

Score: _____ /4

Challenge 2

Use the instructions to find the seven letters of the mystery word. Write the seven-letter below.

- Count 6 backwards from C   ☐

- Opposite V in the mirror line   ☐

- Count 4 forwards from W   ☐

- Opposite G in the mirror line   ☐

- Opposite S in the mirror line   ☐

- Count 7 forwards from X   ☐

- Opposite I in the mirror line   ☐

The seven-letter word is _____.

Score: _____ /1

What is the rule for each of these number sequences?

a) 2   7   17   32   52   77

_____

b) 4   16   8   64   32   1,024

_____

c) 48   160   24   80   12   40

_____

d) 15   12   17   15   19   18

_____

Problem Solving

In a sequence, there may be **two** patterns at work and they may not necessarily go in the same direction. For example, the first, third and fifth numbers may follow one pattern, while the second, fourth and sixth numbers may follow another.

Score: _____ / 4

Challenge 4

What is the rule for each of these letter sequences?

a) AZ   EV   IR   MN   QJ

_____

b) ZC   XF   TL   LX   VV

_____

Score: _____ / 2

Now Try This!

1. Find the number that continues each sequence.

    a) 5   8   14   26   50   _____

    b) 29   31   23   27   17   23   11   _____

2. Find the next pair of letters in each series.

    a) AZ   EU   IP   MK   QF   _____

    b) LG   OY   PK   SC   TO   _____

Problem Solving

Any of the four operations (+ , −, ÷ or ×) can be used in number sequences.

Score: _____ / 4

Total score _____ / 15

LOW   CONFIDENCE   HIGH

Carrying Out Calculations

Let's Get S-t-r-e-t-c-h-i-n-g!

You may need to carry out calculations where:

- letters are used to represent numbers
- you need to work out how two numbers are related to a third number
- you need to find a missing number to balance one side of an equation to the other.

Challenge 1

Insert brackets into these calculations to make them correct.

a) $84 \div 2 \times 3 + 6 = 20$

b) $11 - 2 \times 4 + 5 = 41$

c) $150 \times 2 - 25 \div 5 = 295$

d) $58 + 12 \div 5 \times 4 = 56$

Problem Solving

Keep in mind the BODMAS (or BIDMAS) rule where there is more than one operation involved: Brackets, Order/Indices, Division and Multipliation, Addition and Subtraction.

Score: _____ / 4

Challenge 2

Look at the numbers in this set.

Draw a square around any square numbers and circle any cube numbers.

24	4	343	144	36
216	56	200	120	8
96	125	225	81	400
9	72	16	121	64
27	49	48	100	25

Top Tip

Make sure you are familiar with square numbers and cube numbers since they could be involved in the relationship between a set of numbers.

Score: _____ / 2

Show **two different** ways that you can use the two outer numbers to produce the number in brackets by applying two mathematical operations.

Problem Solving

In the 11+ test, you might need to use more than one operation to find the middle number.

For example:

10 (8) 5 $10 \div 5 + 6$ $10 - 5 + 3$

a) 7 (60) 8   ....

b) 6 (33) 5   ....

c) 16 (20) 32   ....

Score: _____ /6

Challenge 4

$A = 15$, $B = 30$, $C = 75$, $D = 8$, $E = 20$

Write the correct letters in the boxes to make each calculation correct.

a) ☐ $\div$ ☐ $\times$ ☐ $+$ ☐ $-$ ☐ $= B$

b) (☐ $-$ ☐) $\times$ (☐ $\div$ ☐) $= E$

Score: _____ /2

Now Try This!

1. If $A = 4$, $B = 5$, $C = 12$, $D = 16$, $E = 20$, write the answer to these calculations as a letter.

    a) $(A \times E) \div B - C =$ ....

    b) $E \div B \times A - A =$ ....

2. Find the missing number to complete these equations.

    a) $13 \times 9 - 12 = 330 \div 3 -$ ....

    b) $192 \div 12 \times 3 =$ .... $\div 6 + 16$

3. The three numbers in each set are related in the **same** way.
    Find the number that completes the last set.

    a) (56 [4] 7)   (64 [4] 8)   (84 [.............] 7)

    b) (3 [27] 1)   (2 [64] 2)   (2 [.............] 3)

Score: _____ /6

Total score _____ /20

LOW   CONFIDENCE   HIGH

VR   77

Logic

Let's Get S-t-r-e-t-c-h-i-n-g!

Logic questions test your ability to read and understand information. The information might look quite complicated at first so you need to organise the facts into a form that enables you to answer the question. You may need to identify a statement that must be true or cannot be true, or deduce the answer to a problem.

Top Tip

Remember these measurement conversions:
1,000 g = 1 kg
1,000 m = 1 km
60 seconds = 1 minute
60 minutes = 1 hour

Challenge 1

a) Asif has 10 pairs of blue socks and 10 pairs of white socks in a drawer.

If he closes his eyes, how many times would he have to reach into the drawer to take out a sock to be certain of getting a matching pair?

b) Sol's mother has three children.
The first is called April and the second is called May.

What is the name of the third child?

c) **Statement:** Most of the clothes in the shop are expensive.

   Conclusion: i. There are no cheap clothes in that shop.

   ii. Some clothes are cheap in that shop.

Select one of the options below to show whether you agree with one, both or neither of the statements in the conclusion. Write your answer in the box.

A i only   **B** ii only   **C** Both i and ii   **D** Neither i nor ii

Score: _____ /3

Challenge 2

Use the table below to work out who has the most pets.

Leo has a cat and a dog. Ellis has a goldfish. Sunita has two rabbits, two goldfish and a gerbil. Dav has twice the number of cats as Leo and both he and Ellis own a hamster. Sunita doesn't like either of Leo's pet lizards but likes both his rabbits. Ellis would like to have more than the two gerbils he has but he's not allowed.

Problem Solving

Organise the information you are given, e.g. in a diagram, table or a tally chart.

	Cat	Dog	Rabbit	Goldfish	Hamster	Gerbil	Lizard
Leo							
Ellis							
Sunita							
Dav							

_____ has the most pets.

Score: _____ /1

Henry is Charlie's mother's brother and William is Charlie's father's father. Andrew is William's son. Using this information, decide which of the following statements is true.

A William is Charlie's grandfather

B Charlie is Henry's uncle

C Andrew is William's brother

D Henry is Charlie's brother

E Andrew is Henry's brother

Score: _____ / 1

Challenge 4

a) Claire, Ralf, Parvis, Jake and Nell are chefs competing in a cookery contest. Each chef makes a meal using different ingredients.

Ralf, Parvis and Jake all use potatoes. Four of the chefs use carrots. Nell is the only chef whose meal contains fish; the rest use chicken. Everyone except Parvis uses flour in their sauce. Claire is the only chef not to use salt. Parvis uses onions and mushrooms in his sauce, while Nell opts for just onions.

Top Tip

Double check how many people are involved by re-reading the information you are given.

Which chef uses the fewest ingredients to make their meal? _____

b) Rick has four dogs. One is black, two are brown and one is white. The white and black ones have green eyes. The other two dogs have blue eyes. The blue-eyed dogs wear blue collars.

If these statements are true, only one of the sentences below **must** be true. Which one?

A The dogs all have green eyes.

B The blue-eyed dogs are black and brown.

C The brown dogs have blue eyes.

D The white dog is long-haired.

E The green-eyed dogs wear green collars.

Score: _____ / 2

Now Try This!

Hanami, Anna, Ben, Duncan and Keir are meeting at the train station to go to London. Hanami got to the station half-an-hour after Ben arrived. She was the second person to arrive. Ben got there 45 minutes before Keir. The train left at 7:30 pm. Duncan arrived 10 minutes before Anna. Keir arrived 45 minutes before the train departed. Anna arrived 15 minutes before the train left.

If these statements are true, only **one** of the sentences below must be true. Which one?

A Anna was the fourth person to arrive at the station.

B Keir arrived before Hanami.

C Hanami arrived at 6:30 pm.

D Ben arrived after Duncan.

E Hanami arrived before Ben.

Score: _____ / 1

Total score _____ / 8

LOW CONFIDENCE HIGH

1. Use one word from each box to complete each sentence. (3)

lacklustre	sodden	arid	strong
wet	chivalrous	feeble	absurdity
gallant	inspired	imbecility	dry

_____ is to _____ as _____ is to _____

_____ is to _____ as _____ is to _____

_____ is to _____ as _____ is to _____

2. Try to make 16 words using the letters in the word **vegetable**. (4)

....

....

....

....

3. Write a sentence containing each **homophone** below. (4)

complement ....

compliment ....

affect ....

effect ....

4. Underline the **two words**, one from each set of brackets, that are **closest in meaning**. (1)

(sufficient   plentiful   wealthy)   (scarce   abundant   efficient)

5. Insert the same letter to complete each word and start the next. There are **two** possible answers for each pair. (6)

mas___ ___ilt   fli___ ___ent   plo___ ___rop

mas___ ___ilt   fli___ ___ent   plo___ ___rop

6. Think of a word that could share a meaning with **both** pairs of words in brackets.   (1)

    (yard   inch)   (toe   ankle)

    ....

7. Dev, Stacey and Isaac go to at least one after-school club.
    Dev is in the hockey club but he didn't join the choir with Isaac.
    Stacey doesn't play football.
    Isaac is in the cookery club.

    Which of the following statements **must be true**?   (1)

    A   Isaac is in the choir.
    B   Stacey is in the football club.
    C   Isaac is a good cook.
    D   Dev is a member of two clubs.
    E   Stacey is the only one who doesn't play football.

8. A = 8, B = 7, C = 6, D = 5, E = 4, F = 3, G = 2

    Complete each sum below with a letter.   (2)

    a) $(A \times D) \div E - B =$ ☐

    b) $G \times (E \div A) + 2G =$ ☐

9. Find the missing number to complete the sums.   (2)

    a) $14 \times 8 - 13 = 330 \div 3 -$ ☐

    b) $121 \div 11 + 54 = 7 \times$ ☐ $+ 2$

10. Underline the **two words**, one from each set of brackets, that are **most opposite** in meaning.   (1)

    (dictatorship   kingdom   commonwealth)   (democracy   nation   government)

11. Work out these. The alphabet is here to help you:

    A B C D E F G H I J K L M N O P Q R S T U V W X Y Z   (2)

    a)   **YV** is connected to **BE** by a rule.

        Connect **WU** to a letter pair using the same rule.   ....

    b)   **SV** is connected to **OS** by a rule.

        Connect **LO** to a letter pair using the same rule.   ....

12. A farmer wants to cross a river with a wolf, a goat and a cabbage. He has a boat, but it can only fit himself plus either the wolf, the goat or the cabbage. If the wolf and the goat are left alone on one shore, the wolf will eat the goat. If the goat and the cabbage are alone on the shore, the goat will eat the cabbage.

How can the farmer bring the wolf, the goat and the cabbage across the river without anything being eaten? **(1)**

....

....

13. The number codes for three of these four words are listed below.
Crack the code to answer the questions that follow. **(4)**

ACHE   CASH   CAPE   PEAS

5431   6152   4523

a) Find the code for the word **HEAP**. ....

b) Find the code for the word **CASE**. ....

c) Find the word that has the code **4523**. ....

d) Find the word that has the code **6541**. ....

14. Add **one letter** to each word below to make a completely new word.
Write the new word in the space next to each. **(6)**

a) drive ....   b) plot ....   c) chef ....

d) fame ....   e) potion ....   f) crows ....

15. The alphabet is here to help you with this question.

A B C D E F G H I J K L M N O P Q R S T U V W X Y Z

WS is to **QA** as **HV** is to .... **(1)**

16. Find the next pair of letters in this series. **(1)**

ND   OC   OA   NX   LT   ....

17. Find **one** four-letter word that will complete **all** of the following sentences. (1)

    Ben .... his fishing line into the river.

    Ciara's wardrobe .... a shadow on the floor.

    Dad was .... in the leading role in the play.

    Next year, Randall will be able to .... a vote in the election.

    Joseph .... a glance at his opponent before the whistle blew.

18. What is the rule for creating the second word in these pairs? (1)

    (sittings   sit)   (entrance   eat)   (reproach   hop)

    ....

19. Underline **two words**, one from each set of brackets, that complete the sentence. (2)

    a) **object** is to (disagree   thing   pronoun) as **agree** is to (ensure   concur   occur)

    b) **breath** is to (breadth   broad   breathe) as **thought** is to (think   mind   brain)

20. In each sentence, find **three** four-letter words hidden across the end of one word and the start of the next. (3)

    a) Kate said it interested her to meet people from other countries.

        ....

    b) My new hairdo met all my expectations and I had many compliments.

        ....

    c) My three sisters enjoy singing and are always putting on shows.

        ....

21. Underline the **two words** in each group that are most closely related. (2)

    a) (weary   tentative   demonstrative   wariness   uncertain)

    b) (follow   procure   trail   defer   question)

Total score _____ / 49

LOW   CONFIDENCE   HIGH

VR   83

Let's Get S-t-r-e-t-c-h-i-n-g!

Let's practise identifying relationships between different shapes and figures. You will need to identify a series of similarities and differences to select the best fit for a group.

Top Tip
Two different shapes could have any of these in common:
- Symmetry
- Shading
- Reflection
- Number
- Angles
- How shapes overlap or touch
- Line type
- Rotation
- Size
- Regular/irregular shapes
- Direction of arrows

Challenge 1

Can you identify what the shapes in each set have in common? Draw a further figure for each set that fits the rule linking each group of figures.

a)

b)

Score: _____ / 2

Challenge 2

Waleed is playing with the following letters.

a) Sort the letters into **three** distinct groups using symmetry. What are the rules for grouping them?

_____

_____

b) You may find you have one 'odd one out'. Which letter is it and why?

_____

Score: _____ / 2

Look at these shapes:

Write a rule to show what the shapes have in common.

_____

_____

_____

Score: _____ / 1

Now Try This!

Work out what makes the images on the left similar to each other. Then find the image on the right that is most like the images on the left.

1.

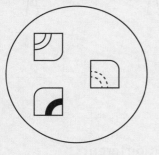

    A   B   C   D   E

2.

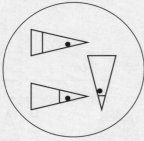

    A   B   C   D   E

3.

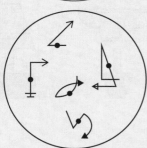

    A   B   C   D   E

4.

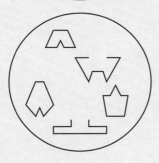   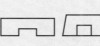

    A   B   C   D   E

Score: _____ / 4

Total score _____ / 9

LOW   CONFIDENCE   HIGH

Let's Get S-t-r-e-t-c-h-i-n-g!

In your 11+ test, you may need to find similarities between a group of figures and identify an 'odd one out'. Look for connections that link all the figures in the group. For example, 'they all have striped shading' or 'they all have dashed lines'. Keep searching for rules that connect all the figures until you find a rule that works for all except one image.

Challenge 1

Bill is a farmer who keeps rare breed chickens. Look at the chickens he has collected for a health check.

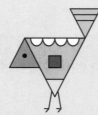 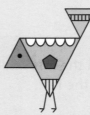 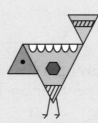 

a) Identify four similarities between the chickens.

_____

_____

b) The fourth chicken is slightly different from the others. In what way is it different?

_____

Score: _____ /2

Challenge 2

Bill also sells topiary trees from the farm. Look at the trees.

A   B   C   D

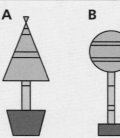 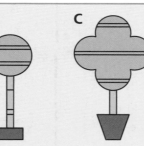 

a) Identify three things that are similar about each tree.

_____

_____

b) Can you find a rule for why each tree could be the odd one out?

_____

_____

_____

Score: _____ /2

Bill has also planted some unusual flowerbeds, as shown below. He loves different varieties of red roses but is very particular about the criteria for each flowerbed.

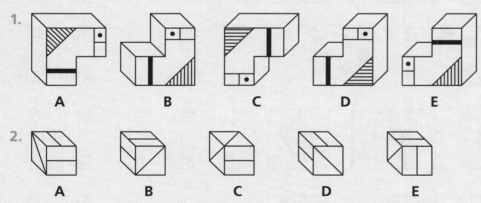

A   B   C

D   E   F

a) Find three similarities between the flowerbeds.

_____

_____

b) Identify two beds which would be different from the others.

_____

c) In the space above, draw two more beds that fit the criteria for Bill's roses.

Score: _____ / 3

Look at each row of five images. Work out which image is most unlike the other four.

1.
A   B   C   D   E

2.
A   B   C   D   E

3.
A   B   C   D   E

Score: _____ / 3

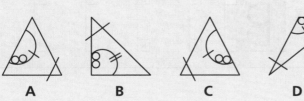

Total score _____ / 10

LOW   CONFIDENCE   HIGH

Let's Get S-t-r-e-t-c-h-i-n-g!

On the next pages, you will be presented with a different type of challenge: code-breaking. These questions require you to look for similarities in the images with the same code letter, then deduce the correct code for the blank figure on the right-hand side of the question.

Challenge 1

Hugo has asked for your help in solving the mystery of his dog Ted's missing collar. All that remains is a note left at the scene of the crime by the perpetrator.

To help solve the mystery, look at the following codes. The images on the left each have a code. Work out how the codes go with these images. Then find the correct code from the list on the right that matches the final image on the right-hand side of the question.

As you decode the figures, write the letters in the spaces in the yellow box at the bottom of page 89, working across the top row first. The top letter of the code for the first figure should be written in the first space in the yellow box, then the second letter of the code for the first figure should be written in the second space. The top letter of the code for the second figure should be written in the third space in the yellow box, and so on. Eventually, the letters will spell out a hidden message.

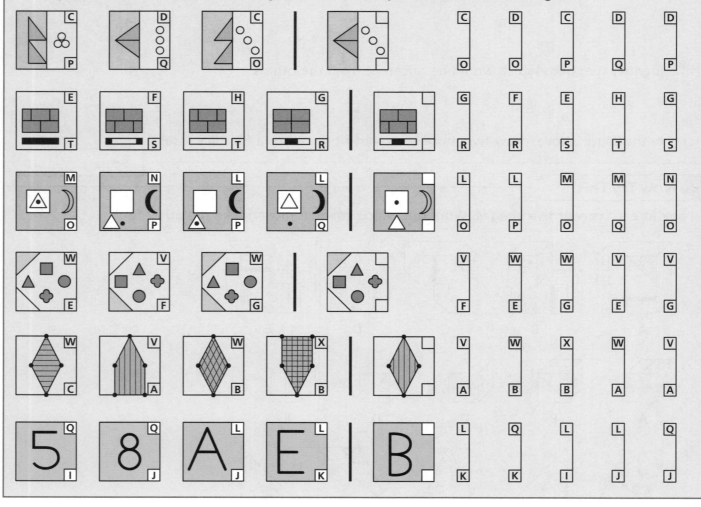

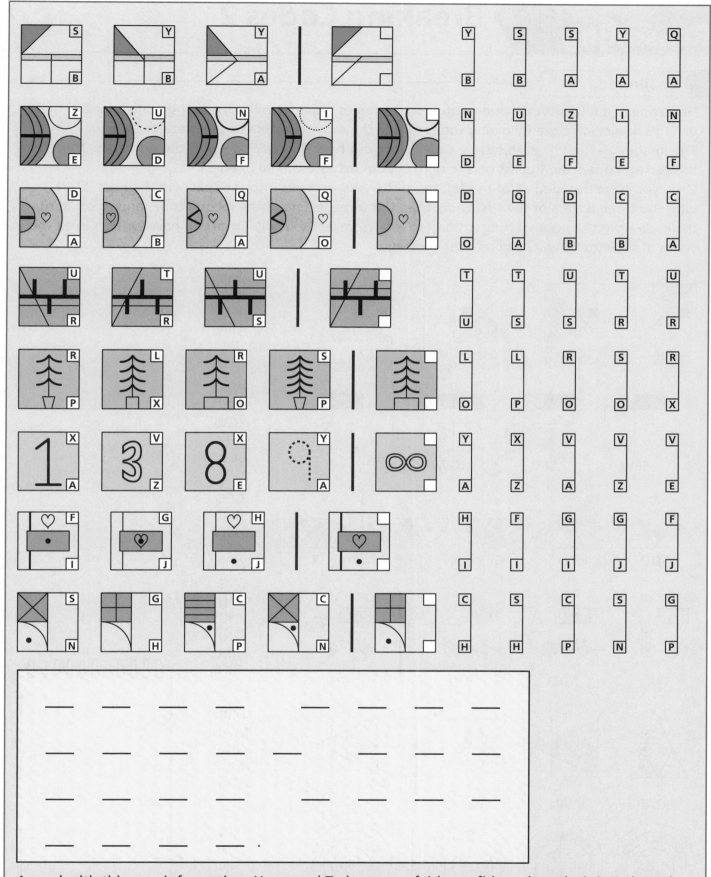

Armed with this new information, Hugo and Ted are now fairly confident the culprit is Ted's arch-enemy, Henry the puzzle-loving poodle. However, they still need to prove it was him. Continue to the next page to find out what challenges lie ahead for them.

Challenge 1

Hugo and Ted find another clue written on a scrap of paper. It will provide the motive for the theft of Ted's collar. Solve the following codes to find the missing letters to complete the note.

The images on the left each have a code. Work out how the codes go with these images. Then find the correct code from the list on the right that matches the final image.

Once you have decoded all of the figures, write your answers into the spaces in the note. Start with the three letters of the first code, then the three letters of the second code, and so on. Write the codes into the note starting at the top left, from left to right. Once you have written in all the codes in order, they will complete the message.

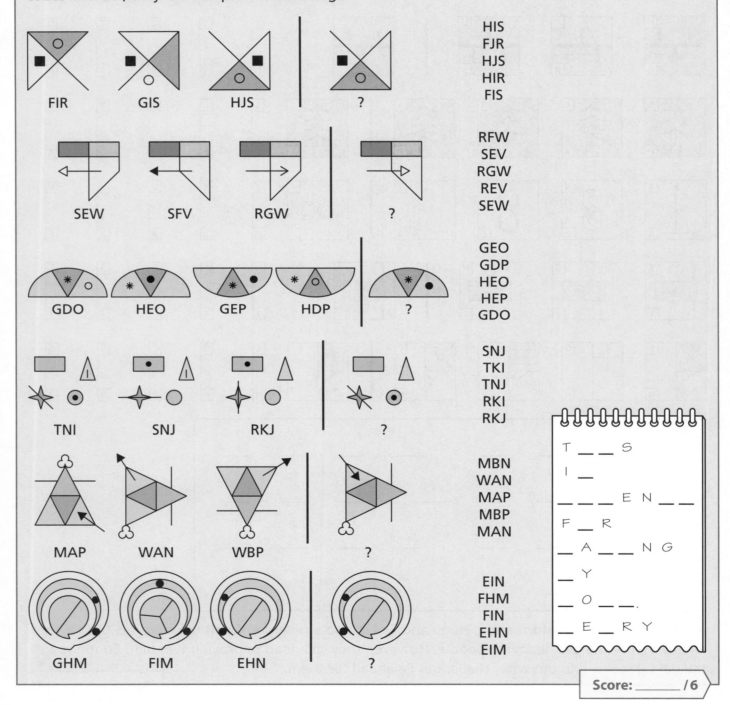

Score: _____ /6

Finally, Hugo and Ted are sure of the culprit. To uncover the location of the collar, solve the following codes and write the code for the figure on the right-hand side of each question on the lines. When put together, the codes will reveal the location of the buried collar.

VNE   VMD   UOD   _ _ _

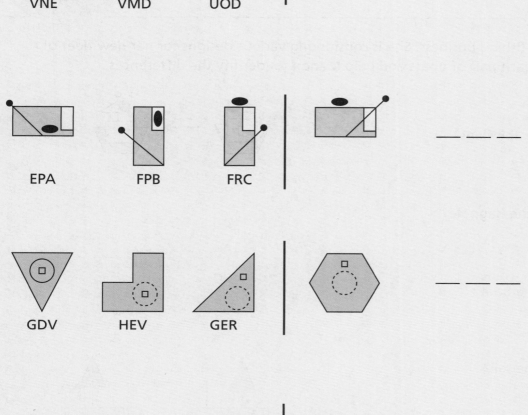

EPA   FPB   FRC   _ _ _

GDV   HEV   GER   _ _ _

TYB   RYA   TNC   _ _ _

USH   XQT   XQH   _ _ _

Write the codes found above in order to reveal the location:

___ ___ ___ ___   ___ ___ ___ ___   ___ ___ ___.

Score: _____ /5

Total score _____ /11

LOW   CONFIDENCE   HIGH

Finding Relationships

Let's Get S-t-r-e-t-c-h-i-n-g!

In the following questions you will need to consider how a figure changes, then apply that rule to other shapes.

Problem Solving

Different parts of each figure will change in different ways.

Challenge 1

Manon has a deep-sea fishing business. She is considering various designs for her new fleet of fishing boats. Look at each pair of boats and help Manon to identify the differences.

Can you find:

a) i) one difference in the flags?

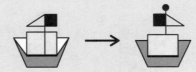

_____

ii) two changes in the flagpole?

_____

iii) one change in the boat?

_____

b) i) one change in the sail?

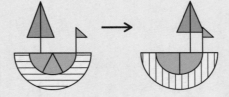

_____

ii) two differences in the boat?

_____

c) i) one change in the flagpole?

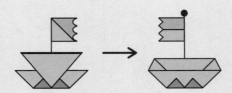

_____

ii) two changes in the flag?

_____

iii) four changes in the boat?

_____

_____

Score: _____ /8

Manon also keeps fish in tanks to investigate the best diet for them. Look at how the first fish in each line has changed after its two-week diet, then draw what the third fish will look like when it has changed in the same way.

Problem Solving

Pay attention to every detail of the image as it changes.

a)

b)

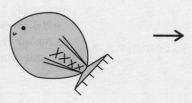
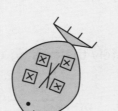
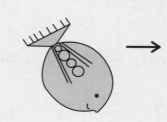

Score: _____ / 2

Challenge 3

Finally, Manon turns her attention to her pet goldfish and the coral she grows for them. Look at the first figure in each line and how it changes into the second figure. Then select the correct figure to show how the third image would change in the same way.

a)

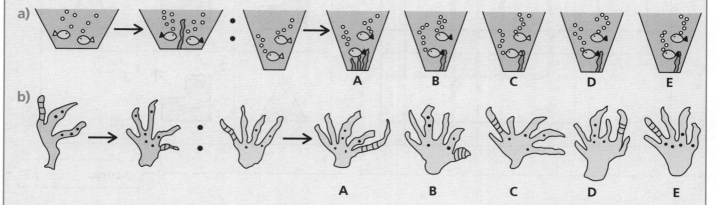

A   B   C   D   E

b)

A   B   C   D   E

Score: _____ / 2

Now Try This!

Decide which image (A, B, C, D or E) goes with the third image to make a pair like the two on the left.

1.

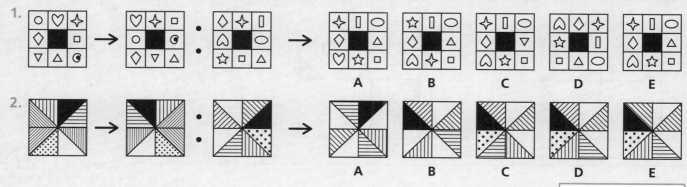

A   B   C   D   E

2.

A   B   C   D   E

Score: _____ / 2

Total score _____ / 14

LOW   CONFIDENCE   HIGH

NVR

93

Let's Get S-t-r-e-t-c-h-i-n-g!

In the following questions, you will need to think about 2 × 2 and 3 × 3 grids with patterns in them. Sometimes the patterns flow between the squares of the grid; at other times, there is a rule or change applied to the squares.

> **Challenge 1**

Karin is a potter creating bespoke tiles for some clients' new kitchens. Help her to complete the patterns she is designing.

Look at the following 3 × 3 grids. Draw accurately the missing tile to complete the grid.

Top Tip

Look for patterns running horizontally, vertically and diagonally in 'complete the grid' questions.

a)

b)

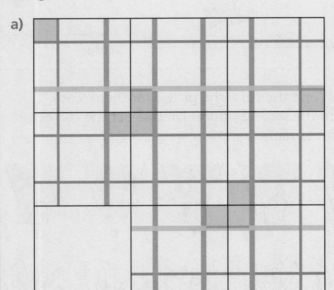

Score: _____ /2

> **Challenge 2**

Karin then creates some smaller 2 × 2 grids with her tile patterns.
Draw a suggestion for each grid to complete the patterns sensibly.

a)

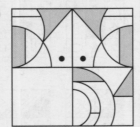

b)

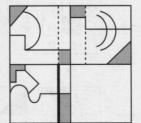

Score: _____ /2

Challenge 3

Karin becomes more ambitious with her tiles and starts to include patterns that work in more complex ways.

In the 3 × 3 grid, the bold lines move position across the rows. The same number of circles appear in each box on the same row and they align along the same side of the box down each row. The division and multiplication signs stay in the same position across the diagonals.

In the 2 × 2 grid, the arrows are related along the rows. They are the mirror image of one another in each row. The curves are related by the columns. They are in the same place in each column.

Now draw your own grids. Make sure you include different elements changing according to the rows, columns and diagonals in each grid.

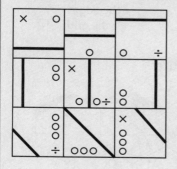 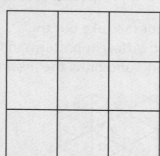 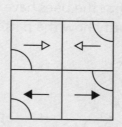 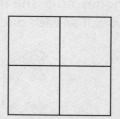

Score: _____ /2

Now Try This!

Work out which of the five boxes on the right completes the grid on the left.

1.

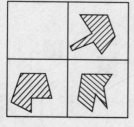

A   B   C   D   E

2.

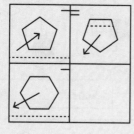

A   B   C   D   E

3.

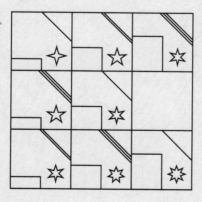

A   B   C   D   E

Score: _____ /3

Total score _____ /9

LOW CONFIDENCE HIGH

NVR   95

Spotting Patterns 2

Let's Get S-t-r-e-t-c-h-i-n-g!

The following patterns include relationships between shapes that flow through different shaped grids.

Problem Solving

Just like in the square grids, look for patterns running horizontally, vertically and diagonally as well as going around the edges of the grid.

Challenge 1

Martha's farm has several beehives. When she goes to take out the honeycomb, she finds that the bees have created different patterns in the wax. For each one, identify how the pattern works and draw the missing figure.

a)

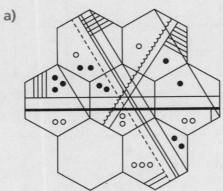

b)

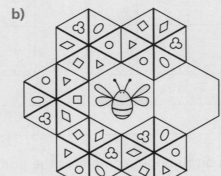

c)

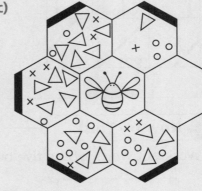

d)

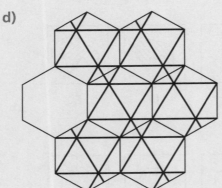

e)

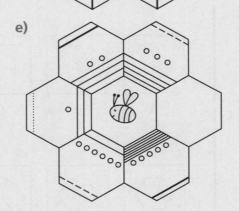

f)

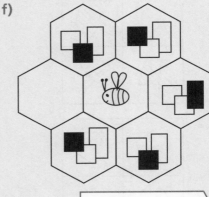

Score: _____ /6

Challenge 2

Martha investigates small sections of the bees' honeycomb. Look at how the patterns are formed in the example on the left-hand side.

Can you draw a pattern for a honeycomb including elements that work in the same ways?

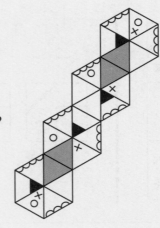

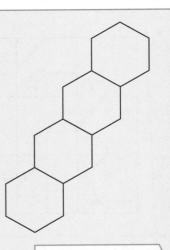

Score: _____ /1

Look at how these octagonal patterns work and draw the missing patterns accurately.

a)

b)

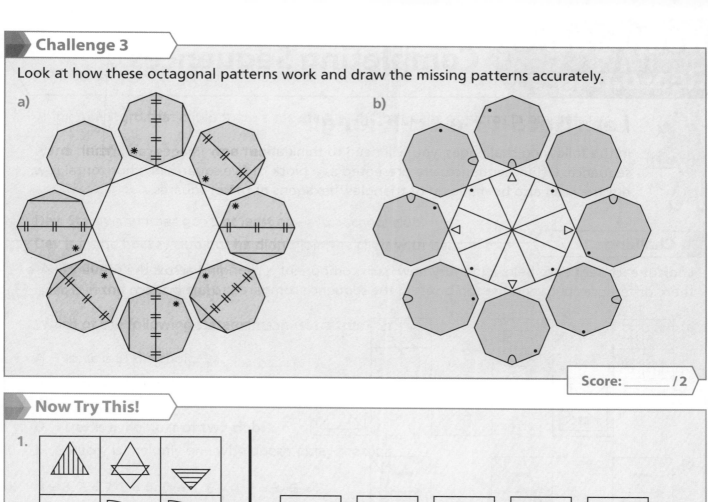

Score: _____ /2

1.

2.

3.

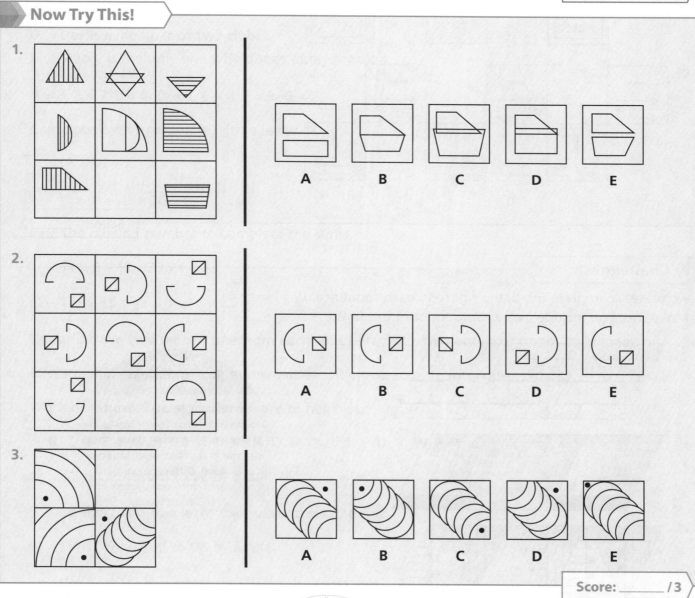

Score: _____ /3

Total score _____ /12

LOW   CONFIDENCE   HIGH

NVR

97

Non-Verbal Reasoning

Completing Sequences

Let's Get S-t-r-e-t-c-h-i-n-g!

In the following challenges, you will need to think about how images can alter in a sequence. Often, sequences are presented as a block of five squares in a horizontal row, but they can also be made up of triangles, hexagons or offset squares.

Challenge 1

Look at each sequence below. Identify how each component is changing across the sequence. Are there differences between the top boxes in the sequence compared to the bottom boxes?

a)
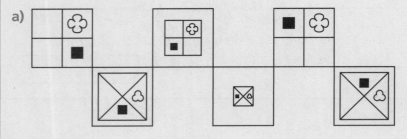

....

....

....

....

b)
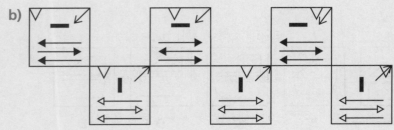

....

....

....

....

Score: _____ /2

Challenge 2

Accurately complete the blank figure in each sequence.
Make sure you include every component in the figure.

a)
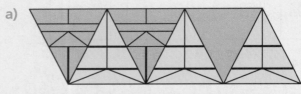

b)
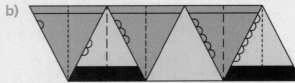

c)
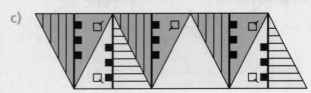

> **Problem Solving**
>
> Sometimes figures alternate between the different boxes in a sequence. At other times, they change in number, orientation or reflection. Different elements of a sequence can change in different ways.

Score: _____ /3

Challenge 3

The hexagonal sequence shown right has several different components:

- The bold circles become increasingly bold working clockwise around the hexagon.
- The crosses alternate between one and two around the hexagon.
- The small circles increase in number working clockwise around the hexagon.

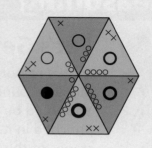

Draw your own hexagonal sequences in the shapes below. Remember to include components which change in different ways.

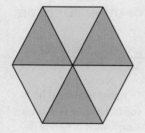 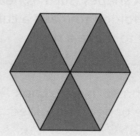 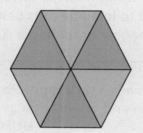

Score: _____ /3

Now Try This!

Look at the five boxes in each question. One of the boxes is empty. One of the five boxes on the right (A, B, C, D or E) should take the place of the empty one. Decide which one.

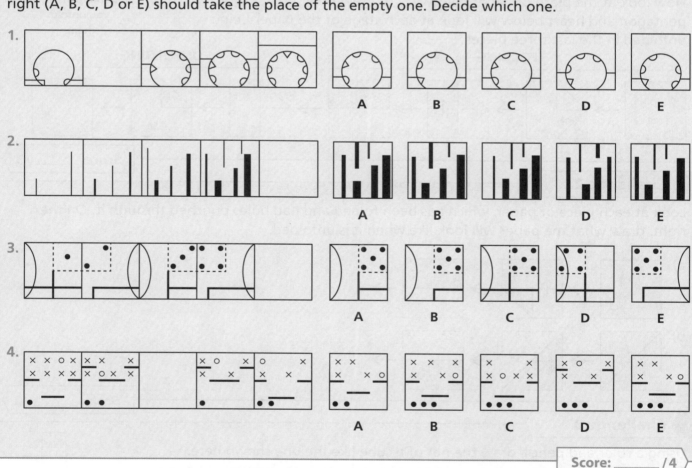

Score: _____ /4

Total score _____ / 12

LOW   CONFIDENCE   HIGH

Let's Get S-t-r-e-t-c-h-i-n-g!

Spatial reasoning involves thinking about how shapes and 3D objects will change when moved around or viewed from different angles.

You could be asked to imagine that a square of paper is being folded up, before holes are punched in it. The hardest questions of this type include holes being punched at different stages of the folding, or using holes of different shapes (such as hearts or hexagons).

You might also be asked to imagine nets being folded to make a cube or other 3D shape; you may also need to imagine unfolding a cube to make a net.

Challenge 1

Shown below is a piece of paper with a different colour on each side. Look at how the heart changes position and orientation as the paper is unfolded:

FOLDING   **UNFOLDING**

Now look at the piece of paper below. Try to draw how the hexagon, pentagon and heart below will look at each stage of the paper being unfolded in the last three pieces.

FOLDING   **UNFOLDING**

Top Tip

Non-circular holes punched in folded paper will look different when it is unfolded. You can practise these skills using folded squares of paper and cutting out different shaped holes to see what happens when you unfold them.

Score: _____ /3

Challenge 2

Look at each piece of paper, which has been folded and had holes punched through it. On the right, draw what the paper will look like when it is unfolded.

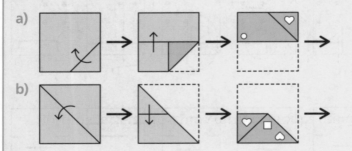

Score: _____ /2

Challenge 3

Using a ruler and pencil, draw the net of a cube like the one shown here:
Then draw a picture on each face. Look at how the pictures rotate, which are opposite one another and how the faces will touch when the cube is folded.
Finally, cut out the cube and fold it along the lines. Were you correct?

You could do the same for the 10 other possible nets of cubes.

Score: _____ /3

For each net, find the pairs of faces which are opposite one another when it is folded into a cube.

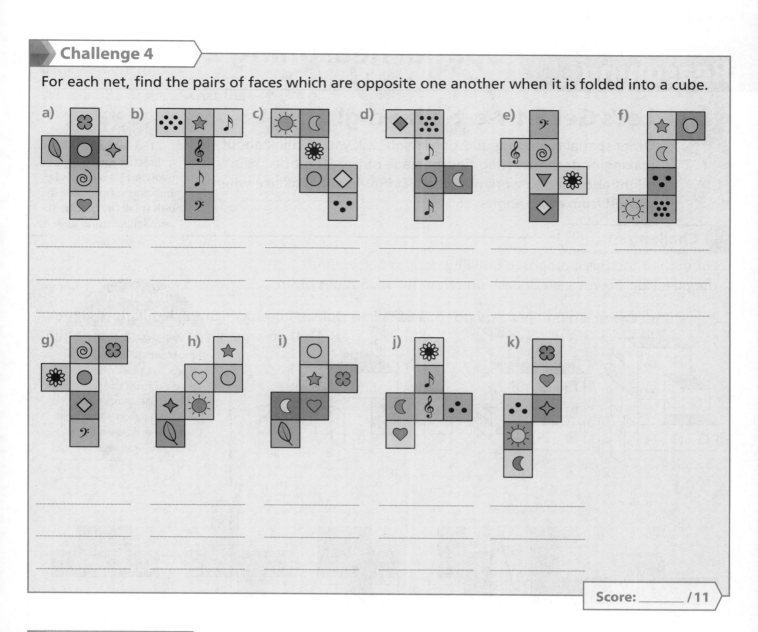

a)
b)
c)
d)
e)
f)

g)
h)
i)
j)
k)

Score: _____ /11

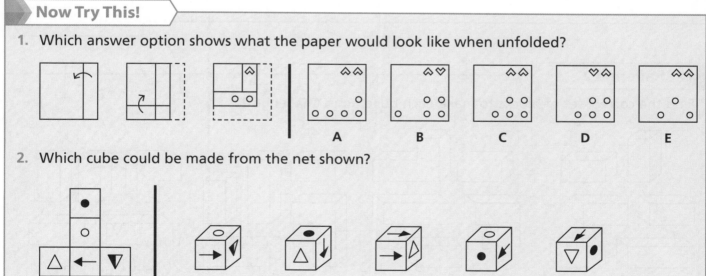

1. Which answer option shows what the paper would look like when unfolded?

A   B   C   D   E

2. Which cube could be made from the net shown?

A   B   C   D   E

Score: _____ /2

Total score _____ /21

LOW   CONFIDENCE   HIGH

Let's Get S-t-r-e-t-c-h-i-n-g!

Other spatial reasoning questions might ask you to think about making or deconstructing figures made out of 3D blocks. You might also need to work out what 3D figures will look like when viewed from other angles.

Top Tip

The best way to practise questions involving 3D blocks is by building some yourself with small toy blocks. 3D modelling using junk is also good!

Challenge 1

For each of the three proposed building designs below, find the plan (top-down) view of each one from the six options given.

Problem Solving

To develop your problem solving skills, draw the view of each building from the right-hand side. Work out which building has the smallest area on its right-hand side.

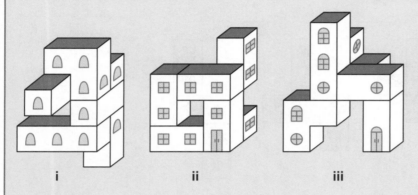

i ii iii

A B C D E F

Score: _____ /3

Challenge 2

Find the correct set of blocks to make each building in Challenge 1.

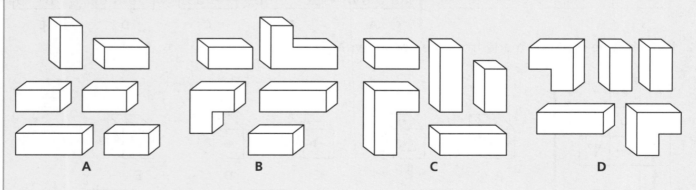

A B C D

Building **i**: ☐   Building **ii**: ☐   Building **iii**: ☐

Score: _____ /3

Oliver has been playing with his toy bricks.
He has made the following scene.
Draw the plan (top-down) view of each of
the four sets of blocks using the grid below.

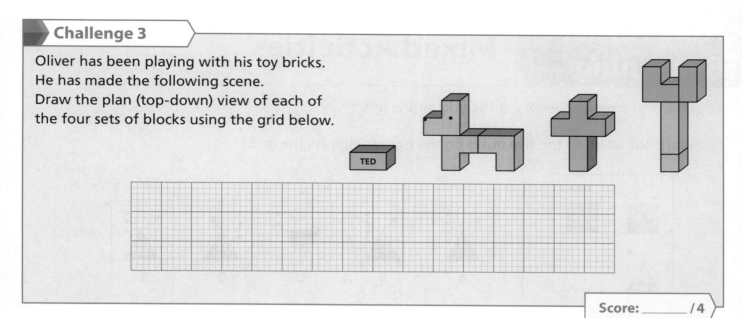

TED

Score: _____ / 4

Now Try This!

Which set of blocks (A, B, C, D or E) can be used to create each 3D model?

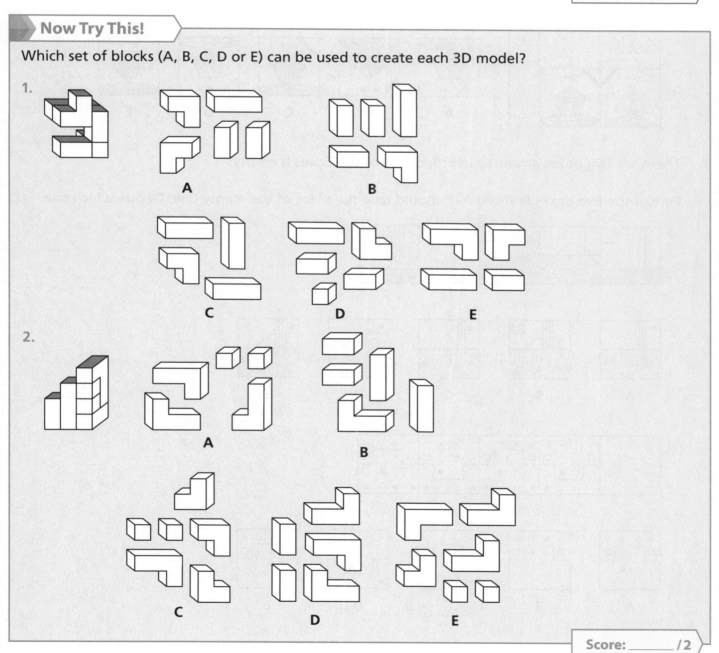

1.

A

B

C

D

E

2.

A

B

C

D

E

Score: _____ / 2

Total score _____ / 12

LOW   CONFIDENCE   HIGH

1. One of the boxes is empty in the grid on the left.

   Work out which of the five boxes on the right completes the grid. (2)

a)

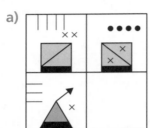

   A   B   C   D   E

b)

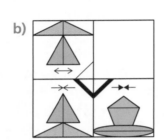

   A   B   C   D   E

2. There are five boxes arranged in order. One of the boxes is empty.

   One of the five boxes labelled A–E should take the place of the empty one. Decide which one. (2)

a)

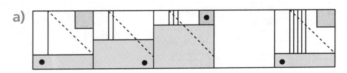

   A   B   C   D   E

b)

   A   B   C   D   E

3. The four images on the left each have a code. Work out how the codes go with these images. Then look at the image on the right of the vertical line and find its code from the five options given. (2)

a)

     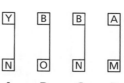

A   B   C   D   E

b)

     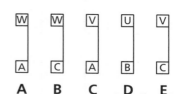

A   B   C   D   E

4. There are two images on the left with an arrow between them. Then there is a third image with an arrow pointing to five more images labelled A–E. Decide which one of these five images goes with the third image to make a pair like the two above. (2)

a)

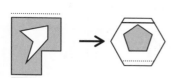

 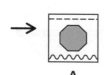

   A   B   C   D   E

b)

 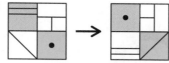

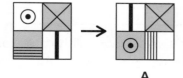

   A   B   C   D   E

5. Work out what makes the two images on the left similar to each other. Then find the image on the right that is most like the two images on the left.

(2)

a)

    A   B   C   D   E

b)

    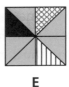

    A   B   C   D   E

6. Look at the line of five images. Work out which image is most unlike the other four.

(2)

a)

  A   B   C   D   E

b)

  A   B   C   D   E

7. Look at the given cube. Work out which net could be folded to make the cube. (2)

a)

 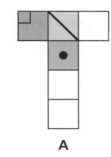 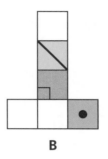 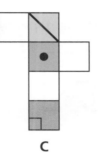 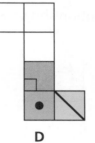 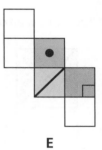

                      A   **B**   **C**   **D**   **E**

b)

 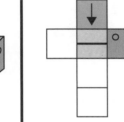 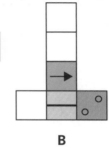 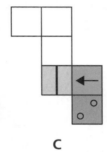 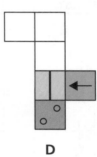 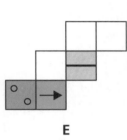

                      A   **B**   **C**   **D**   **E**

8. Match shapes i, ii and iii to their correct rotations A, B and C. (2)

         i   **ii**   **iii**

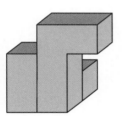 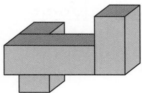 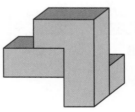

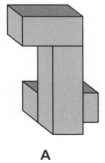 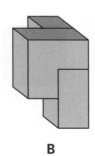 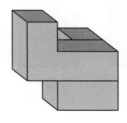

         A   **B**   **C**

9. Look at the paper below, which is folded before holes are punched through it.

Which answer option shows what the paper would look like when unfolded? (3)

a)

   A   **B**   **C**   **D**   **E**

b)

    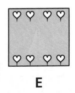

   A   **B**   **C**   **D**   **E**

c)

   A   **B**   **C**   **D**   **E**

LOW   CONFIDENCE   HIGH

Collins

Mathematics

Test Paper

Read these instructions carefully:

1. You must not open or turn over this booklet until you are told to do so.

2. This booklet is a multiple-choice test containing different types of questions.

3. Do all rough working on a separate sheet of paper.

4. You should mark your answers in pencil on the answer sheet provided, not on this booklet.

5. Rub out any mistakes as well as you can and mark your new answer.

6. Try to do as many questions as you can. If you find that you cannot do a question, do not waste time on it but go on to the next one.

7. If you are stuck on a question, choose the answer that you think is best.

8. You have 50 minutes to complete the test.

1 Work out two thousand four hundred and three multiplied by three.

A 7,290   B 2,409   C 7,353   D 2,947   E 7,209

2 62.45 × 193.2 = 12,065.34

Calculate **624.5 × 1.932**

A 120.6534   B 1,206.534   C 12,065.34   D 12.06534   E 120,653.4

3 Three friends counted how many soft toys they owned and recorded the results in this pictogram.

Ranjeet

Colin

Pete

= 6 toys

What is the mean number of soft toys owned by the friends?

A 3   B 20   C 18   D 16   E 24

4 What number finishes this sequence?

                    –4, 19, 15, 34, …

A 42   B 43   C 41   D 49   E 50

5 **What percentage of this shape is shaded?**

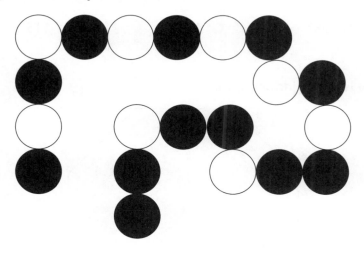

A 75%   B 65%   C 55%   D 60%   E 70%

6 Add 15% of £2 to a quarter of £6.

How much money do you end up with?

A £1.80   B £2   C £1.75   D £1.90   E £2.10

7 **What is the missing number in this calculation?**

574 × ☐ = 0.574

A 0.01   B 0.001   C 0.0001   D 0.1   E 0.0101

8 Liam arrives at work at 8:34 am. The walk from his house to the bus stop is 18 minutes.

The bus journey is 37 minutes and the walk from the bus stop to his work is 13 minutes.

At what time did Liam leave his house?

A 7:29 am   B 7:30 am   C 7:26 am   D 7:34 am   E 7:25 am

9 What is the angle between the two hands of a clock at 2:30?

    A 125°   **B** 95°   **C** 110°   **D** 115°   **E** 105°

10 The shape below is a regular octagon.

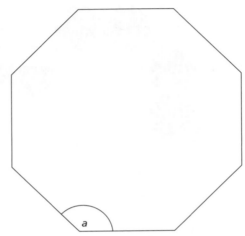

What is the size of angle *a*?

    A 80°   **B** 150°   **C** 135°   **D** 125°   **E** 145°

11 A water tank measures 6 m long, 1 m high and 1 m wide.

How many litres of water will the tank hold?

    A 6 litres   **B** 6,000 litres   **C** 600 litres   **D** 60,000 litres   **E** 0.6 litres

12 What are the prime numbers between 80 and 90?

    A 83 and 89   **B** 81 and 87   **C** There aren't any   **D** 83 and 85   **E** 86 and 89

13 On the grid below, plot the coordinates A (3, 2), B (2, 4) and C (4, 4) to make a triangle. Now reflect that triangle in the *y*-axis.

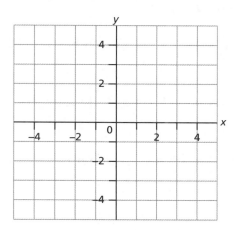

What are the new coordinates of point C after the reflection?

A (−2, 4)   **B** (−4, 4)   **C** (4, −4)   **D** (3, 4)   **E** (2, −4)

14 Sasha works in the local shop. She gets paid £8.50 per hour and a 5% commission on everything she sells. Over the weekend she worked 14 hours and sold £564 worth of products.

How much did she earn in total over the weekend?

A £138.20   **B** £152.40   **C** £145.60   **D** £147.20   **E** £144.80

15 **What is 68.32 − 19.39?**

A 47.33   **B** 50.03   **C** 48.93   **D** 48.83   **E** 48.97

16 Angles *a* and *b* lie on a straight line and are in the ratio of 3 : 1.

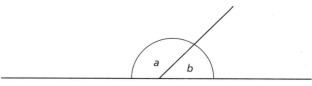

What is the size of angle *a*?

A 135°   **B** 125°   **C** 140°   **D** 145°   **E** 150°

17 Liam is facing directly North East. He turns 90 degrees clockwise.

What direction is he facing now?

A South   B South West   C South East   D North West   E East

18 Peter needs to fill his fish tank with 120 litres of water. He is using a container that holds 400 ml.

How many times will he need to fill his container in order to fill the fish tank to his requirements?

A 30   B 3   C 3,000   D 300   E 330

19 Aaron is looking at his train timetable. He is travelling from London to Newcastle and he chooses the train that has the shortest journey time. However, once on the train there is a delay of 37 minutes before he gets to his destination.

Station	Train 1	Train 2
Bournemouth	0703	0935
London	0815	1049
Birmingham	1022	1228
Newcastle	1348	1503

How long did he spend on the train?

A 4 hours 59 minutes

B 5 hours 7 minutes

C 4 hours 46 minutes

D 4 hours 51 minutes

E 4 hours 45 minutes

20 Which of these 3D shapes has 5 faces, 9 edges and 6 vertices?

A hemisphere

B cuboid

C regular tetrahedron

D square-based pyramid

E triangular prism

21 What is the perimeter of the shape below? It is not drawn to scale.

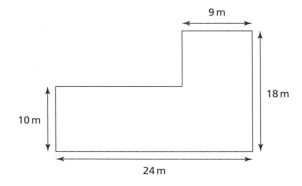

A 61 m   B 76 m   C 84 m   D 90 m   E 124 m

22 Calculate the area of the shape in question 21.

A 240 m²   B 362 m²   C 520 m²   D 312 m²   E 402 m²

23 On Sunday, I went for a run. After 3 miles I stopped for a rest. I still had three-fifths of my run to go, which I went on to complete.

How far was my run from start to finish?

A 7.5 miles   B 7 miles   C 21 miles   D 8 miles   E 8.5 miles

Maths Practice Paper

24 Poonam is looking at the menu in the café. She decides to buy 3 packets of crisps, 2 sandwiches and a soup.

```
            Menu

Crisps          80p
Sandwiches      £1.45
Rolls           £1.75
Soup            £1.90
```

How much change does she get back from £10?

A £2.95   **B** £2.80   **C** £3.05   **D** £2.65   **E** £3.10

25 The graph below shows the miles travelled by the Jones family on their leisurely Sunday walk. They left at 7:00 am.

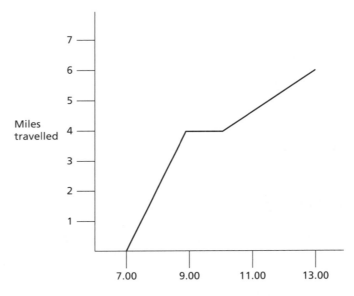

How long did they stop for breakfast?

A 30 minutes   **B** 45 minutes   **C** 10 minutes   **D** 1 hour   **E** 20 minutes

26 Using the graph from question 25, what was the Jones family's average speed across their whole walk?

A 1 mph   **B** 1.5 mph   **C** 3 mph   **D** 5 mph   **E** 2.5 mph

27 I made a huge pizza for my friends. They ate four-sevenths of it. I then ate three-fifths of what remained.

How much pizza was left?

A $\frac{9}{35}$ B $\frac{6}{35}$ C $\frac{1}{4}$ D $\frac{1}{3}$ E $\frac{2}{9}$

28 **What is the volume of this box in cubic metres?**

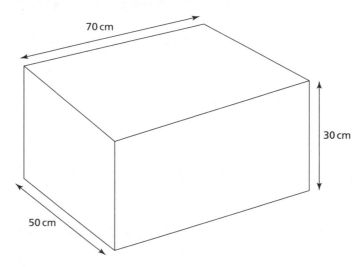

70 cm

30 cm

50 cm

A 105,000 m³   B 10.5 m³   C 105 m³   D 0.105 m³   E 1.05 m³

29 The patio in my garden is a perfect square. It has a width of 7 m.

What is the perimeter of the patio?

A 49 m   B 14 m   C 28 m   D 35 m   E 21 m

30 Karim got 72 marks in his test, which was 60% of the marks available.

What was the total number of marks available?

A 135   B 120   C 130   D 115   E 110

31 Which of these numbers is closest to 2?

1.9909   2.0012   1.9099   2.0919   1.0999

A 1.9909   B 2.0012   C 1.9099   D 2.0919   E 1.0999

32 What is the next number in this sequence?

8, 64, 512, ...

A 572   B 576   C 960   D 5,046   E 4,096

33 This number machine takes an INPUT number, multiplies it by 5, adds 75, then halves the result.

What was the INPUT if the OUTPUT is 125?

A 45   B 50   C 35   D 30   E 25

34 Wayne goes to the shop and buys 4 cans of cola and 5 pencils for £3.65.

He then returns to the shop and buys 2 cans of cola and 6 pencils for £2.70.

How much is one pencil in the shop?

A 15p   **B** 35p   **C** 40p   **D** 25p   **E** 30p

35 Sally has four times as many books as Guy. Aled has twice as many books as Sally.

The three friends have 195 books between them.

How many books does Sally have?

A 60   **B** 70   **C** 50   **D** 55   **E** 65

36 The table below shows the contents of three friends' piggy banks.

What should be in the blank space in the table?

	20p coins	50p coins	£1 coins	TOTAL
Virat	9	6	3	£7.80
Joe	16	3	4	£8.70
Ros	34		7	£23.30

A 16   **B** 17   **C** 18   **D** 19   **E** 20

Maths Practice Paper

37 Pauline is going to tile her bathroom. The area she wants to tile has a width of 35 cm and a height of 40 cm. The tiles she is going to use measure 70 mm × 20 mm.

How many tiles will she need?

A 10   B 100   C 1,000   D 500   E 250

38 1 foot is 30.5 cm and 1 inch is 2.5 cm. I am 6 foot 3 inches.

What is my height in metres?

A 1.895 m   B 1.91 m   C 1.9 m   D 1.89 m   E 1.905 m

39 Steve has been saving up to buy a computer in the sale. It was £1,350 but has been reduced by 20% in the sale.

If he has already saved £720, how much more money will he need in order to buy the computer in the sale?

A £420   B £380   C £350   D £360   E £390

40 Here is part of a shape with a vertical line of symmetry.

Which shape is made by completing it with the given line of symmetry?

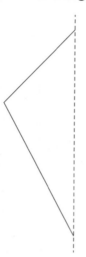

A square   **B** kite   **C** triangle   **D** pentagon   **E** hexagon

41 **If April 21ˢᵗ is a Wednesday, what day is May 21ˢᵗ?**

A Wednesday   **B** Thursday   **C** Friday   **D** Saturday   **E** Sunday

42 Twenty-three years ago my grandmother was 68. I am 74 years younger than my grandmother.

How old was I twelve years ago?

A 17   **B** 3   **C** 5   **D** 6   **E** 12

43 The employees at a company were surveyed on how they got to work that morning. The results are shown in this pie chart, which is not drawn to scale.

226 said they got there by car.

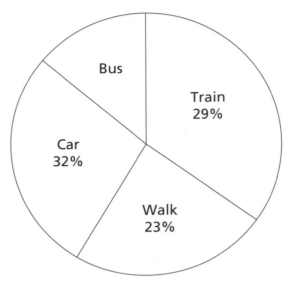

How many took the bus?

A 120   B 110   C 115   D 113   E 125

44 What is the next number in this sequence?

126, 93, 59, 24, ...

A −12   B 6   C 2   D 0   E −14

45 Calculate 13 + (9 × 5) − 7 + (8 × 6)

A 696   B 666   C 99   D 95   E 82

46 Bahrain is two hours ahead of the UK. Angus took a flight from the UK to Bahrain which landed at 11:47 pm local time.

If the flight time was 6 hours and 24 minutes, what was the local time in London when his plane took off?

A 5:23 pm   **B** 3:23 pm   **C** 7:23 pm   **D** 1:47 am   **E** 4:23 pm

47 Find the expression for the perimeter of this rectangle:

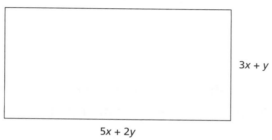

$3x + y$

$5x + 2y$

A $15x + 2y$ **B** $15x + 3y$ **C** $16x + y$ **D** $16x + 6y$ **E** $15x + 2y^2$

48 Find the expression for the area of the rectangle in question 47.

A $15x^2 + 11xy + 2y^2$ **B** $15x + 2y$ **C** $15x^2 + 4y^2$ **D** $15x^2 + 4y$ **E** $16x + 6y$

49 Chris can paint $3\,m^2$ in 15 minutes.

How long will it take him to paint a cube with a side length of $3\,m$?

A   15 minutes

B   4 and a half hours

C   4 hours

D   6 and a half hours

E   2 and a half hours

50 Using only prime numbers in the hundreds and units values and only a square number in the tens value, what is the highest three-digit number you can make?

A 797   B 999   C 979   D 777   E 747

END OF PAPER

Collins

English

Test Paper

Read these instructions carefully:

1. You must not turn over this page until you are told to do so.

2. This paper contains a passage for you to read and some questions for you to answer. You can refer to the passage to check your answers as many times as you want. You will then need to complete some spelling, punctuation and grammar exercises.

3. This is a multiple-choice test, so select your answer from the options on the answer sheet. Mark only **one** answer for each question.

4. Make sure you draw a line firmly through the rectangle next to your answer. If you make a mistake, rub it out as much as you can and mark your new answer.

5. Try to answer as many questions as you can. If you find that you cannot answer a question, do not waste time on it but simply go on to the next one. If you are not sure of an answer, choose the option that you think is best.

6. Do all rough working on a separate sheet of paper.

7. You have 50 minutes to complete the test.

Comprehension

Read this passage carefully, then answer the questions.

The Signalman

Charles Dickens

> *In the story, the narrator sees a signalman, who works on the railway line.*

1 "Halloa! Below there!"

When he heard a voice thus calling to him, he was standing at the door of his box, with a flag in his
hand, furled round its short pole. One would have thought, considering the nature of the ground,
that he could not have doubted from what quarter the voice came; but instead of looking up to
5 where I stood on the top of the steep cutting nearly over his head, he turned himself about, and
looked down the Line. There was something remarkable in his manner of doing so, though I could
not have said for my life what. But I know it was remarkable enough to attract my notice, even
though his figure was foreshortened and shadowed, down in the deep trench, and mine was high
above him, so steeped in the glow of an angry sunset, that I had shaded my eyes with my hand
10 before I saw him at all.

"Halloa! Below!"

From looking down the Line, he turned himself about again, and, raising his eyes, saw my figure
high above him.

"Is there any path by which I can come down and speak to you?"

15 He looked up at me without replying, and I looked down at him without pressing him too soon
with a repetition of my idle question. Just then there came a vague vibration in the earth and air,
quickly changing into a violent pulsation, and an oncoming rush that caused me to start back,
as though it had force to draw me down. When such vapour as rose to my height from this rapid
train had passed me, and was skimming away over the landscape, I looked down again, and saw
20 him refurling the flag he had shown while the train went by.

I repeated my inquiry. After a pause, during which he seemed to regard me with fixed attention,
he motioned with his rolled-up flag towards a point on my level, some two or three hundred yards
distant. I called down to him, "All right!" and made for that point. There, by dint of looking closely
about me, I found a rough zigzag descending path notched out, which I followed.

25 The cutting was extremely deep, and unusually precipitate. It was made through a clammy stone,
that became oozier and wetter as I went down. For these reasons, I found the way long enough to
give me time to recall a singular air of reluctance or compulsion with which he had pointed out
the path.

When I came down low enough upon the zigzag descent to see him again, I saw that he was
30 standing between the rails on the way by which the train had lately passed, in an attitude as if he
were waiting for me to appear. He had his left hand at his chin, and that left elbow rested on his
right hand, crossed over his breast. His attitude was one of such expectation and watchfulness that
I stopped a moment, wondering at it.

I resumed my downward way, and stepping out upon the level of the railroad, and drawing nearer
35 to him, saw that he was a dark, sallow man, with a dark beard and rather heavy eyebrows. His post
was in as solitary and dismal a place as ever I saw. On either side, a dripping-wet wall of jagged
stone, excluding all view but a strip of sky; the perspective one way only a crooked prolongation
of this great dungeon; the shorter perspective in the other direction terminating in a gloomy red
light, and the gloomier entrance to a black tunnel, in whose massive architecture there was a
40 barbarous, depressing, and forbidding air. So little sunlight ever found its way to this spot, that it
had an earthy, deadly smell; and so much cold wind rushed through it, that it struck chill to me, as
if I had left the natural world.

Before he stirred, I was near enough to him to have touched him. Not even then removing his
eyes from mine, he stepped back one step, and lifted his hand.

45 This was a lonesome post to occupy (I said), and it had riveted my attention when I looked down
from up yonder. A visitor was a rarity, I should suppose; not an unwelcome rarity, I hoped? In me,
he merely saw a man who had been shut up within narrow limits all his life, and who, being at last
set free, had a newly-awakened interest in these great works. To such purpose I spoke to him; but I
am far from sure of the terms I used; for, besides that I am not happy in opening any conversation,
50 there was something in the man that daunted me.

He directed a most curious look towards the red light near the tunnel's mouth, and looked all
about it, as if something were missing from it, and then looked at me.

That light was part of his charge? Was it not?

He answered in a low voice,—"Don't you know it is?"

55 The monstrous thought came into my mind, as I perused the fixed eyes and the saturnine face,
that this was a spirit, not a man. I have speculated since, whether there may have been infection in
his mind.

In my turn, I stepped back. But in making the action, I detected in his eyes some latent fear of me.
This put the monstrous thought to flight.

60 "You look at me," I said, forcing a smile, "as if you had a dread of me."

"I was doubtful," he returned, "whether I had seen you before."

"Where?"

He pointed to the red light he had looked at.

"There?" I said.

65 Intently watchful of me, he replied (but without sound), "Yes."

"My good fellow, what should I do there? However, be that as it may, I never was there, you may swear."

"I think I may," he rejoined. "Yes; I am sure I may."

His manner cleared, like my own. He replied to my remarks with readiness, and in well-chosen

70 words. Had he much to do there? Yes; that was to say, he had enough responsibility to bear; but exactness and watchfulness were what was required of him, and of actual work—manual labour— he had next to none. To change that signal, to trim those lights, and to turn this iron handle now and then, was all he had to do under that head. Regarding those many long and lonely hours of which I seemed to make so much, he could only say that the routine of his life had shaped itself

75 into that form, and he had grown used to it.

Now answer these questions. Look back at the passage if you need to.

Choose the best answer and mark its letter on your answer sheet.

1 **What is the 'cutting' in line 5?**

    A Natural undulation in the landscape

    B Trimmings from the bushes

    C An acerbic remark made in conversation

    D The railway line itself

    E An embankment for the train to run through higher ground

2 **What is unusual about the signalman's response to the visitor in the first paragraph?**

    A The narrator cannot tell anything is unexpected in the signalman's response

    B The signalman looks in a different direction to the speaker

    C The speaker doesn't expect him to turn around

    D The signalman should not usually be by his door at that time

    E The signalman would not often be holding a flag

3 **What was the signalman's appearance like when the visitor first saw him?**

A   He was elongated and shaded

B   He was silhouetted and, due to perspective, seemed shorter

C   It was difficult to make him out with clarity

D   He was illuminated by the dusk light

E   He was dishevelled and uneasy

4 **How does the signalman answer the narrator's enquiry?**

A   The rush of the train means he does not reply

B   He says, "All right!"

C   He ignores the narrator entirely

D   He makes a gesture

E   He refurls the flag

5 **What is the path to the signalman's box like?**

A   Impossible to see clearly due to the weather

B   Stony and rough

C   Steep and slippery

D   Level

E   Crooked and depressing

6 **What do we learn about the signalman in lines 29–35?**

A   His face is unhealthy-looking and he is highly alert

B   He has both arms crossed over his chest, each hand resting on an elbow

C   He had a grumpy attitude

D   He does not expect to receive a visitor

E   He has an imposing presence

7   Re-read the phrase 'the shorter perspective in the other direction terminating in a gloomy red light'. What does the writer mean by this?

    A   It was difficult to make out anything on the horizon from the signalman's post

    B   You could not see as far into the distance towards the sunset

    C   The lights of the railway signals were glowing in the dusk

    D   The red light is a metaphor representing the place the narrator came from

    E   You could not see as far into the distance toward the tunnel's mouth

8   What does the visitor say to the signalman?

    A   He thinks the signalman will want to see him, as the signalman is fascinated by him

    B   He presumes the job is isolating; therefore, he is hopeful of being welcome

    C   He is sorry, as there is no novelty in having callers

    D   He hopes the signalman will find him good company

    E   He hopes the signalman is often lonely

9   How does the visitor feel when he sees the signalman's hut?

    A   Fascinated, as he has previously had a very sheltered existence

    B   Horrified, as the box is like a dungeon

    C   Nervous, as the signalman is extremely ill at ease

    D   He is overwhelmed as he sees a man who has been shut up in his box all his life

    E   He has always been interested in projects like railway building

10   What impression do we form of the signalman in lines 55–58?

    A   We see he is highly nervous and may be mentally ill

    B   We realise he is actually a phantom

    C   We realise something dreadful has happened to him in the past

    D   He is a forceful and compelling character

    E   He has led a cloistered life to date and has been limited in what he could do

11 Which description best fits the nature of the signalman's work?

A It requires extremely long working hours

B He has complete control over that section of the railway

C Mentally taxing but physically light

D Physically demanding and highly stressful

E He is overwhelmed with responsibility

12 How does the signalman feel about his work?

A He is shaping his work into what he wants it to be

B He has become accustomed to the isolation

C He has grown to enjoy working entirely alone

D Over time he feels he has matured and developed

E He finds the work extremely lonely and isolating

13 Overall, what atmosphere is created in the story?

A Unnerving and ominous

B Mysterious

C Lackadaisical

D Horrifying

E Scandalous

14 What technique has the writer used in lines 40–42?

A Colloquial language

B Personification

C Metaphor

D Emotive language

E Sensory description

15 Why does the visitor want to talk to the signalman in the extract?

    A We are not told

    B He feels sorry for the lonely signalman

    C He has an interest in the railways

    D He is lonely

    E He has time to spare

16 How do the men feel when it is established that they have not seen one another before (lines 66–69)?

    A Confused

    B Embarrassed

    C Relieved

    D Outraged

    E Anxious

17 What person has the passage been narrated in?

    A First person

    B Second person

    C Third person

    D We do not know

    E The signalman

18 Which word is closest in meaning to 'precipitate' in line 25?

    A Moist   **B** Steep   **C** Impetuous   **D** Imprudent   **E** Crumbly

19 What do 'these great works' refer to in line 48?

    A The trains that pass by the signalman's box

    B The building of the railway tunnel

    C The signalman's great devotion to his duties

    D The processes involved with the railways; industrialisation

    E The visitor's charitable endeavours with working men

20 Re-read line 65. Why does the signalman reply to the narrator 'without sound'?

A He has lost his voice due to ill health

B He is terrified of what might be about to happen

C The signalman and the narrator have an understanding so they do not need to speak to communicate

D He does not want to speak to the narrator as he is unfriendly

E The signalman never speaks to visitors

21 Which word is closest in meaning to 'saturnine' in line 55?

A Sombre   B Miserly   C Contemptible   D Subliminal   E Insubstantial

22 Which word is closest in meaning to 'latent' in line 58?

A Obvious   B Evident   C Dormant   D Overwhelming   E Significant

23 What parts of speech are the following words, as used in the text?

'post'   'watchfulness'   'exactness'   'signal'

A Pronouns   B Adjectives   C Verbs   D Nouns   E Prepositions

24 What parts of speech are the following words, as used in the text?

'foreshortened'   'shadowed'   'steeped'

A Pronouns   B Adjectives   C Verbs   D Nouns   E Prepositions

25 'Only a crooked prolongation…'

What part of speech is 'prolongation'?

A Noun   B Determiner   C Article   D Pronoun   E Verb

English Practice Paper

Spelling

In these sentences there are some spelling mistakes. On each numbered line there is either one mistake or no mistake. Find the group of words with the mistake in it and mark its letter on your answer sheet. If there is no mistake, mark N.

26 Without further ado, we ascended the gallery via the exscalator and began our tour.
      A   B   C   D

27 The erruption that ensued when I voiced my opinion to the committee was unbelievable.
      A   B   C   D

28 Freya's unwavering refusal to answer the question was tantamount to an addmission of guilt.
      A   B   C   D

29 Mum has been dithering about whether we're aloud to pitch the tent in the back garden.
      A   B   C   D

30 Despite the stalwart support of their fans, the singers couldn't clinch a deel with the agent.
      A   B   C   D

31 A somber mood descended on the explorers as they considered their rather limited options.
      A   B   C   D

32 Abdul swiftly installed the most up-to-date anti-virus softwear on his new laptop.
      A   B   C   D

33 The mood was solemn as the head teacher announced her forthcoming retirement.
      A   B   C   D

Punctuation

In this passage there are some punctuation mistakes. On each numbered line there is either one mistake or no mistake. Find the group of words with the mistake in it and mark its letter on your answer sheet. If there is no mistake, mark N.

34 Archie and Leona went deeper into the cave. It's stalagmites and stalactites were a pointed
  A   B   C   D

35 reminder that they were still not out of danger. The drip; drip, drip of water from the back
  A   B   C   D

36 made them thirsty. "Do you think the waters safe to drink?" asked Archie hopefully.
  A   B   C   D

37 "Well have to drink something or we won't be able to carry on," responded Leona.
  A   B   C   D

38 She focused the faint light of her torch towards the sound. A small pool had formed on the
  A   B   C   D

39 caves floor and they lay on their stomachs like animals to lap up the water. Suddenly, there
  A   B   C   D

40 was a distant rumble; Then the mouth of the cave was lit up by a flash of forked
  A   B   C   D

41 lightning. "We will have to bed down here for the night", said Leona miserably.
  A   B   C   D

English Practice Paper

Grammar

In this passage you have to choose the best word, or group of words, to complete each numbered line so that it makes sense and is correctly written in English. Choose from one of the five answer options on each line and mark its letter on your answer sheet.

42 The bank manager | did take | took | was taken | had taken | taken be |
                                  A   B   C   D   E

43 completely unawares; the 'sweet, old lady', | whom | which | whose | what | who |
                                               A   B   C   D   E

44 he had just served, proved to be anything | other | else | at | such | but | ;
                                       A   B   C   D   E

45 he had counted out | his | their | my | there | her | money, which she immediately
                           A   B   C   D   E

46 secured in her bag, then, | in | to | with | at | under | his complete surprise, she
                           A   B   C   D   E

47 produced a gun! "I'll have | the | that | a | an | this | bit more of that, young
                            A   B   C D   E

48 man," she | whispered | did whisper | whispers | was whispering | is whispering |.
                      A   B   C   D   E

49 "You | ought | should | could | would | may | never underestimate an old lady!"
                A   B   C   D   E

END OF PAPER

Collins

Verbal Reasoning
Test Paper

Read these instructions carefully:

1. You must not open or turn over this booklet until you are told to do so.

2. This booklet is a multiple-choice test containing different types of questions.

3. Each question type begins with an explanation, usually followed by an example.

4. Do all rough working on a separate sheet of paper.

5. You should mark your answers in pencil on the answer sheet provided, not on this booklet.

6. You may have to mark more than one answer (you will be told this in the instructions for the question type). Draw a line firmly through the rectangle next to your answer.

7. Rub out any mistakes as well as you can and mark your new answer.

8. Try to do as many questions as you can. If you find that you cannot do a question, do not waste time on it but go on to the next one.

9. If you are stuck on a question, choose the answer that you think is best.

10. You have 50 minutes to complete the test.

Verbal Reasoning Practice Paper

The alphabet is shown here to help you with these questions.

A B C D E F G H I J K L M N O P Q R S T U V W X Y Z

You need to work out a different code or word for each question.

Choose the correct answer and mark it on the answer sheet.

Example

If the code for **SAIL** is **QCGN,** what is the code for **BOAT**?

A ZPYV   B ZQYV   C DMCR   D ZRYV   E YQYV

Answer B ZQYV

1 If the code for **BLOW** is **CNRA**, what is the code for **HORN**?

   A JQRU   B GMOD   C IQUR   D IRUX   E IUQR

2 If the code for **PLAYER** is **KOZBVI**, what is the code for **STADIUM**?

   A NRFWHZG   B ZFBWGH   C NWFRGH   D FRWZHG   E HGZWRFN

3 If the code for **CROWD** is **XNLUC**, what does **LQBSD** mean?

   A QUIET   B CHOIR   C QUAIL   D QUEUE   E QUITE

4 If the code for **PLANET** is **PIUESE**, what does **UOUEID** mean?

   A SATURN   B URANUS   C GEMINI   D COMETS   E APOLLO

5 If the code for **TURKEY** is **UTSJFX**, what is the code for **CHICKEN**?

   A DGJBLDO   B DIHDJFM   C JGHDMFD   D XFJGLOD   E DGDBLOI

6 If the code for **EIGHTY** is **BLDKQB**, what is **KLKHQB** the code for?

   A FOURTY   B NINETY   C TWENTY   D THIRTY   E TWELVE

In each question, find the number that continues the sequence in the most sensible way. Mark the letter for that number on the answer sheet.

Example

99   88   78   69   61   [?]

A 54   B 55   C 53   D 56   E 52

Answer   A   54

7

8   60   7   44   6   30   5   18   4   [?]

A 10   B 12   C 8   D 6   E 2

8

1   1   2   6   24   [?]

A 100   B 48   C 120   D 96   E 72

9

39   12   33   15   28   19   24   24   [?]

A 20   B 23   C 22   D 31   E 21

10

6   8   11   16   23   34   47   [?]

A 60   B 64   C 58   D 57   E 56

11

4   5   9   14   23   [?]

A 34   B 37   C 36   D 24   E 46

12

4   9   25   49   121   [?]

A 190   B 170   C 157   D 169   E 168

Three of these four words are given in code.

The codes are **not** necessarily written in the same order as the words and one code is missing.

ALSO	LEAN	LATE	LOSE
5237	2581	2731	

Choose the correct answer and mark it on the answer sheet.

13 Find the code for the word **LEAN**.

A 2195　　　B 5237　　　C 2581　　　D 2159　　　E 2731

14 Find the word that has the number code **2738**.

A ALSO　　　B TEAL　　　C SOLE　　　D LOSE　　　E LOST

15 Find the code for the word **SLANT**.

A 32598　　　B 32798　　　C 35298　　　D 32589　　　E 32895

Three of these four words are given in code.

The codes are **not** necessarily written in the same order as the words and one code is missing.

NEST	SEAT	HATE	THAN
4365	2536	6431	

Choose the correct answer and mark it on the answer sheet.

16 Find the code for the word **NEST**.

A 1256　　　B 4365　　　C 6431　　　D 1526　　　E 1652

17 Find the word that has the number code **5326**.

A THAT　　　B NEST　　　C EAST　　　D HENS　　　E TEAS

18 Find the code for the word **ATHENS**.

A 643125　　　B 364512　　　C 325612　　　D 361245　　　E 364521

In these sentences, a word of **four letters** is hidden across the **end** of one word and the **beginning** of the next word. Find the pair of words that contains the hidden word and mark its letter on the answer sheet.

Example

It didn't occur to me to invite Hayley to my birthday party.

A didn't occur   **B** occur to   **C** to invite   **D** Hayley to   **E** my birthday

Answer   B occur to

---

19   I told Ciara I'd meet her after the performance.

    A told Ciara   **B** meet her   **C** her after   **D** after the   **E** the performance

20   My dad is German yet he speaks very little of his native language.

    A My dad   **B** German yet   **C** he speaks   **D** little of   **E** native language

21   When I finished my writing, I edited it carefully.

    A finished my   **B** my writing   **C** I edited   **D** edited it   **E** it carefully

22   During the interval everyone queued up to order a drink.

    A During the   **B** the interval   **C** interval everyone   **D** queued up   **E** to order

23   The driver of the school bus knows me very well.

    A driver of   **B** the school   **C** bus knows   **D** knows me   **E** very well

24   The cable dangled dangerously from the ceiling.

    A The cable   **B** cable dangled   **C** dangled dangerously   **D** from the   **E** the ceiling

Verbal Reasoning Practice Paper

These questions show three pairs of words. Find the word that completes the last pair of words in the **same way** as the other two pairs. Mark its letter on the answer sheet.

Example

(honour hour)   (latent lent)   (defame [?])

A fame   B made   C deaf   D feed   E dame

Answer E dame

25 (desserts stressed)   (emit time)   (deliver [?])

    A reviled   B relived   C livered   D derived   E revealed

26 (currant arc)   (glitter tig)   (blunder [?])

    A dub   B red   C bun   D den   E end

27 (gagged aged)   (stable tale)   (orange [?])

    A gran   B rage   C gear   D gone   E roan

28 (painter print)   (broader broad)   (bloomer [?])

    A gloom   B drone   C broom   D loner   E bloom

29 (courage gear)   (primate team)   (orderly [?])

    A lyer   B lord   C load   D lyre   E lore

30 (manger rage)   (porter rote)   (runner [?])

    A near   B rune   C earn   D runt   E turn

31

Read the following information, then find the correct answer to the question and mark it on the answer sheet.

Ronan, Ted, Willow, Sorcha and Andrew all take part in a sponsored race.

Ted didn't finish last.

Andrew finished before Ronan.

Willow finished after Ronan, who came second.

Sorcha finished before Ted.

If these statements are true, only one of the sentences below **must** be true.

Which one?

A   Ronan finished after Willow.

B   Ted came third.

C   Andrew came second.

D   Sorcha finished before Ronan.

E   Willow finished last.

Verbal Reasoning Practice Paper

In these questions, the same letter must fit into both sets of brackets, to complete the word in front of the brackets and begin the word after the brackets. Find this letter and mark it on the answer sheet.

Example

bus [?] ink   cran [?] ind

A t   **B** k   **C** p   **D** s   **E** y

Answer B k

32 mani [?] airn   ar [?] oarse

A c   **B** k   **C** s   **D** h   **E** d

33 chale [?] himble   per [?] arnish

A s   **B** v   **C** c   **D** t   **E** h

34 brin [?] haki   chal [?] elp

A t   **B** e   **C** k   **D** g   **E** h

35 stripe [?] odel   medle [?] earning

A l   **B** s   **C** r   **D** d   **E** y

36 spaw [?] ourish   spur [?] uance

A n   **B** t   **C** q   **D** d   **E** l

37 pro [?] awn   car [?] otent

A d   **B** t   **C** f   **D** l   **E** p

In these questions, letters stand for numbers. Work out the answer to each sum and find its letter. Then mark it on the answer sheet.

Example

If A = 7, B = 9, C = 12, D = 14 and E = 18, what is the answer to this sum **written as a letter**?

$D \times B \div E + A = $ [?]

A A   **B** B   **C** C   **D** D   **E** E

Answer D D

38 If A = 6, B = 9, C = 12, D = 24, E = 36, what is the answer to this sum **written as a letter**?

$E \div C \times A - B = $ [?]

A A   **B** B   **C** C   **D** D   **E** E

39 If A = 3, B = 11, C = 12, D = 18, E = 28, what is the answer to this sum **written as a letter**?

$A \times C - B + A = $ [?]

A A   **B** B   **C** C   **D** D   **E** E

40 If A = 27, B = 12, C = 18, D = 14, E = 4, what is the answer to this sum **written as a letter**?

$A \times B \div C - D = $ [?]

A A   **B** B   **C** C   **D** D   **E** E

41 If A = 7, B = 20, C = 14, D = 36, E = 30, what is the answer to this sum **written as a letter**?

$A \times (C \div A) + D - E = $ [?]

A A   **B** B   **C** C   **D** D   **E** E

42 If A = 4, B = 9, C = 12, D = 16, E = 7, what is the answer to this sum **written as a letter**?

$(C \times B + A) \div E = $ [?]

A A   **B** B   **C** C   **D** D   **E** E

43 If A = 12, B = 13, C = 3, D = 17, E = 35, what is the answer to this sum **written as a letter**?

$(A \times B) \div C - D = $ [?]

A A   **B** B   **C** C   **D** D   **E** E

Verbal Reasoning Practice Paper

The alphabet is shown here to help you with these questions.

A B C D E F G H I J K L M N O P Q R S T U V W X Y Z

Find the letters that will complete the sentence in the best way and mark your answer on the answer sheet.

Example

TS is to QP as BA is to [?]

A YX   B XW   C ZY   D WX   E XY

Answer **A** YX

44 HS is to LO as EV is to [?]

    A DW   B RI   C IS   D JR   E IR

45 BV is to GA as XD is to [?]

    A DA   B CI   C DW   D DU   E EV

46 VW is to ED as XY is to [?]

    A CB   B ZA   C BC   D AB   E BA

47 GT is to MN as BY is to [?]

    A IJ   B JI   C GT   D HS   E GS

48 KY is to WS as QE is to [?]

    A CY   B DZ   C DY   D EW   E EK

49 ME is to NV as DG is to [?]

    A TW   B ZW   C VX   D WY   E WT

In these questions, find **two** words, **one** from each set, that are **most opposite in meaning**. Mark both words on the answer sheet.

(broach pendant surge)   (suggest suppress badge)

A broach   **X** suggest
B pendant   **Y** suppress
C surge   **Z** badge

Answer A broach   **Y** suppress

50 (careful courageous considerate)   (tactless brave private)

A careful   **X** tactless
B courageous   **Y** brave
C considerate   **Z** private

51 (sanction forbid misinform)   (prohibit permit distract)

A sanction   **X** prohibit
B forbid   **Y** permit
C misinform   **Z** distract

52 (intrigue inhibit grace)   (bore draw disgrace)

A intrigue   **X** bore
B inhibit   **Y** draw
C grace   **Z** disgrace

53 (brazen confused stubborn)   (blunt compliant brash)

A brazen   **X** blunt
B confused   **Y** compliant
C stubborn   **Z** brash

54 (forfeit withhold goal)   (penalty reward retain)

A forfeit   **X** penalty
B withhold   **Y** reward
C goal   **Z** retain

55 (brunt faithful adhere)   (tense strong disloyal)

A brunt   **X** tense
B faithful   **Y** strong
C adhere   **Z** disloyal

Verbal Reasoning Practice Paper

In these questions, find **two** words, **one** from each set, that are **closest in meaning**. Mark both words on the answer sheet.

Example

(desperate impetuous courageous)

A desperate
B impetuous
C courageous

Answer B impetuous

(rash clueless cautious)

X rash
Y clueless
Z cautious

X rash

56 (yield conceal bracket)

A yield
B conceal
C bracket

(hinge expose relinquish)

X hinge
Y expose
Z relinquish

57 (deficit extra earnings)

A deficit
B extra
C earnings

(benefit charge surplus)

X benefit
Y charge
Z surplus

58 (block avoid overthink)

A block
B avoid
C overthink

(anxiety address intercept)

X anxiety
Y address
Z intercept

59 (figure count letter)

A figure
B count
C letter

(amount integer model)

X amount
Y integer
Z model

60 (monitor coach watch)

A monitor
B coach
C watch

(horses time mentor)

X horses
Y time
Z mentor

61 (herd boast pride)

A herd
B boast
C pride

(modesty satisfaction lions)

X modesty
Y satisfaction
Z lions

In these questions, find the **two** words, **one** from each set, that will complete the sentence in the best way. Mark **both** words on the answer sheet.

Example

Truck is to (cabin   goods   handbrake) as **ship** is to (stern   anchor   berth).

A cabin
B goods
C handbrake

X stern
Y anchor
Z berth

Answer C handbrake

Y anchor

62

Student is to (exams   degree   university) as **politician** is to (law   parliament   diplomacy).

A exams
B degree
C university

X law
Y parliament
Z diplomacy

63

Graft is to (toil   cut   skin) as **belt** is to (brace   punch   trousers).

A toil
B cut
C skin

X brace
Y punch
Z trousers

64

Calf is to (leg   rhinoceros   ankle) as **kid** is to (goat   child   sheep).

A leg
B rhinoceros
C ankle

X goat
Y child
Z sheep

65

Vein is to (artery   blood   mirror) as **tree** is to (bark   climb   sap).

A artery
B blood
C mirror

X bark
Y climb
Z sap

66

Astronomer is to (gaze   stars   spaceships) as **botanist** is to (plants   space   animals).

A gaze
B stars
C spaceships

X plants
Y space
Z animals

67

Knit is to (needles   wool   brow) as **shrug** is to (carpet   forehead   shoulders).

A needles
B wool
C brow

X carpet
Y forehead
Z shoulders

Verbal Reasoning Practice Paper

The alphabet is shown here to help you with these questions.

A B C D E F G H I J K L M N O P Q R S T U V W X Y Z

Find the next pair of letters in the series and mark it on the answer sheet.

68 DL   GJ   CI   FI   BJ   [?]

A EL   **B** LE   **C** JB   **D** FE   **E** LJ

69 PQ   SS   QP   TR   RO   [?]

A TT   **B** QR   **C** UQ   **D** SQ   **E** TU

70 CC   BE   ZD   WF   SE   [?]

A TG   **B** NG   **C** XF   **D** MF   **E** NF

71 TT   YP   CM   FK   HJ   [?]

A JK   **B** LN   **C** IK   **D** IH   **E** IJ

72 QR   RQ   OQ   PR   MT   [?]

A MX   **B** NX   **C** LW   **D** NW   **E** NV

73 DL   GJ   CI   FI   BJ   [?]

A FH   **B** EL   **C** FL   **D** GL   **E** EK

In these questions, the three numbers in each set are related in the **same** way. Find the number that completes the last set and mark it on the answer sheet.

Example

(3 [24] 9)   (8 [34] 9)   (14 [?] 9)

A 64   B 46   C 63   D 45   E 44

Answer B 46

74

(18 [12] 3)   (24 [19] 7)   (36 [?] 9)

A 27   B 4   C 29   D 18   E 26

75

(12 [6] 3)   (16 [8] 4)   (27 [?] 3)

A 7   B 18   C 9   D 8   E 10

76

(5 [16] 26)   (8 [15] 31)   (2 [?] 23)

A 17   B 18   C 21   D 19   E 15

77

(24 [8] 3)   (27 [18] 6)   (45 [?] 5)

A 28   B 23   C 26   D 27   E 25

78

(27 [16] 9)   (56 [20] 8)   (96 [?] 12)

A 21   B 23   C 8   D 25   E 19

79

(5 [135] 9)   (7 [168] 8)   (9 [?] 12)

A 216   B 324   C 328   D 218   E 326

80 Read the statements below, then find the correct answer to the question and mark it on the answer sheet.

Audrey, Pedro, Dan, Sonny and Ella visit a zoo.

Four of the children hold a boa constrictor.

Pedro is the only who doesn't touch the tarantula.

Audrey, Dan and Ella take turns to hold the green and black poison frog.

Sonny holds all the creatures apart from the boa constrictor and the poison frog.

Audrey and Sonny have their picture taken holding the tarantula and a bearded lizard.

No-one except Pedro holds the gecko or the meerkat.

Which child touches the fewest creatures in the zoo?

A Audrey   **B** Pedro   **C** Dan   **D** Sonny   **E** Ella

END OF PAPER

Non-Verbal Reasoning
Test Paper

Read these instructions carefully:

1. You must not open or turn over this booklet until you are told to do so.

2. The booklet contains a multiple-choice test, in which you have to mark your answer to each question on the separate answer sheet.

3. There are five sections in this test. Each section starts with an explanation of what to do, followed by an example. You will then be asked to do some practice questions. Explanations of the answers for these are included.

4. You should indicate one answer only for each question by drawing a firm pencil line clearly through the rectangle next to your answer on the answer sheet. Rub out any mistakes as well as you can and put in your new answer.

5. Complete the questions as quickly and as carefully as you can. If you find that you cannot do a question, do not waste time on it but go on to the next one.

6. You have 6 minutes to complete the 12 questions in each section.

7. You should do any rough working on a separate sheet of paper.

Section 1

Look at the given net on the left. Work out which one of the cubes on the right can be made using that net.

Example

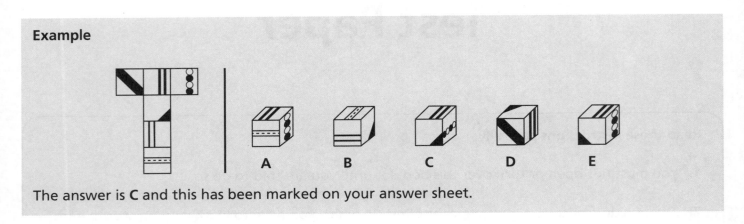

The answer is **C** and this has been marked on your answer sheet.

Now do the two practice questions below.

P1

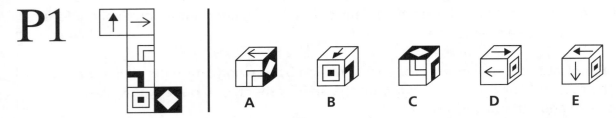

The answer is **C**. Mark this answer in Practice Question 1 for Section 1 on your answer sheet.

P2

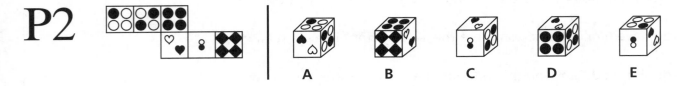

The answer is **A**. Mark this answer in Practice Question 2 for Section 1 on your answer sheet.

> **You now have 6 minutes to complete the next 12 questions.**

1

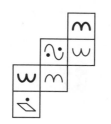

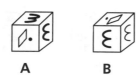

A B C D E

2

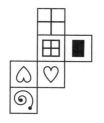

A B C D E

3

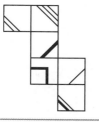

A B C D E

4

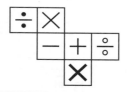

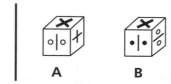

A B C D E

5

A B C D E

6

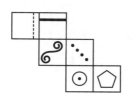

A B C D E

7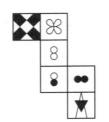

A   **B**   **C**   **D**   **E**

8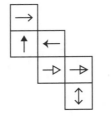

A   **B**   **C**   **D**   **E**

9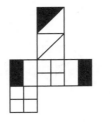

A   **B**   **C**   **D**   **E**

10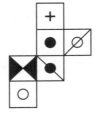

A   **B**   **C**   **D**   **E**

11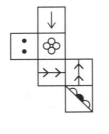

A   **B**   **C**   **D**   **E**

12

A   **B**   **C**   **D**   **E**

Section 2

Look at the line of five images. Work out which image is **most unlike** the other four.

 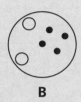  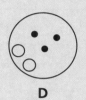 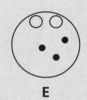
Now do the two practice questions below.

P1

A B C D E

The shape most unlike the others is **D** because in all the other figures, the crosses are aligned vertically. Mark the answer **D** in Practice Question 1 for Section 2 on your answer sheet.

P2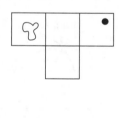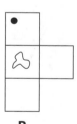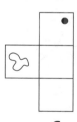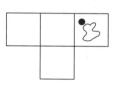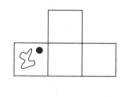

A B C D E

The shape most unlike the others is **C**. In all the other figures, if the T-shapes were rotated to look like a T, the black dot would be in the top right-hand corner. Mark the answer **C** in Practice Question 2 for Section 2 on your answer sheet.

You now have 6 minutes to complete the next 12 questions.

1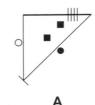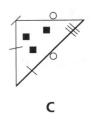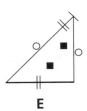

A   B   C   D   E

2

A   B   C   D   E

3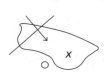

A   B   C   D   E

4

A   B   C   D   E

5

A   B   C   D   E

6

A   B   C   D   E

7

A   B   C   D   E

8

A   B   C   D   E

9

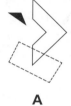  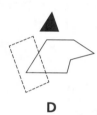

A   B   C   D   E

10

A   B   C   D   E

11

A   B   C   D   E

12

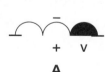   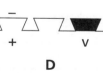 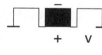

A   B   C   D   E

Section 3

Look at the shape on the left. The shape is hidden in one of the five images on the right. Find which image contains the given shape.

Example

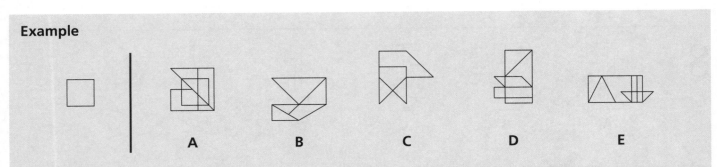

The hidden figure can be rotated but not reflected, and must be the same size as the shape shown on the left-hand side of the question. Therefore, the hidden shape is in option **A**. This has been marked on your answer sheet.

Now do the two practice questions below.

P1

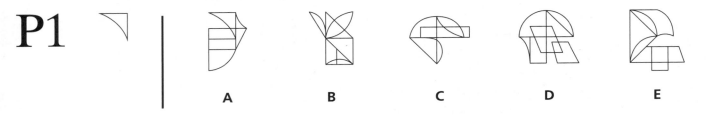

The figure is hidden in option **A**. Mark the answer **A** in Practice Question 1 for Section 3 on your answer sheet.

P2

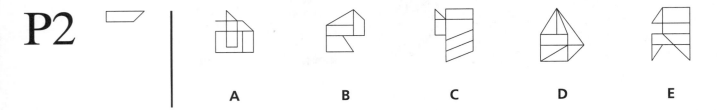

The figure is hidden in option **A**. Mark the answer **A** in Practice Question 2 for Section 3 on your answer sheet.

You now have 6 minutes to complete the next 12 questions.

1

A   B   C   D   E

2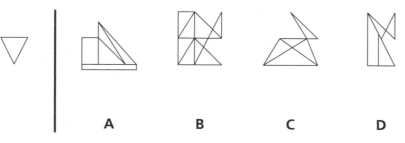

A   B   C   D   E

3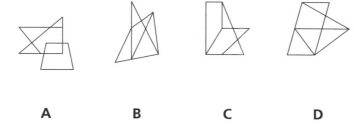

A   B   C   D   E

4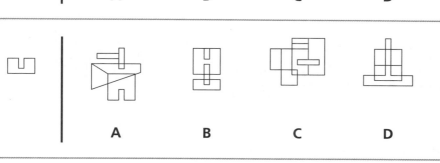

A   B   C   D   E

5

A   B   C   D   E

6

A   B   C   D   E

Non-Verbal Reasoning Practice Paper

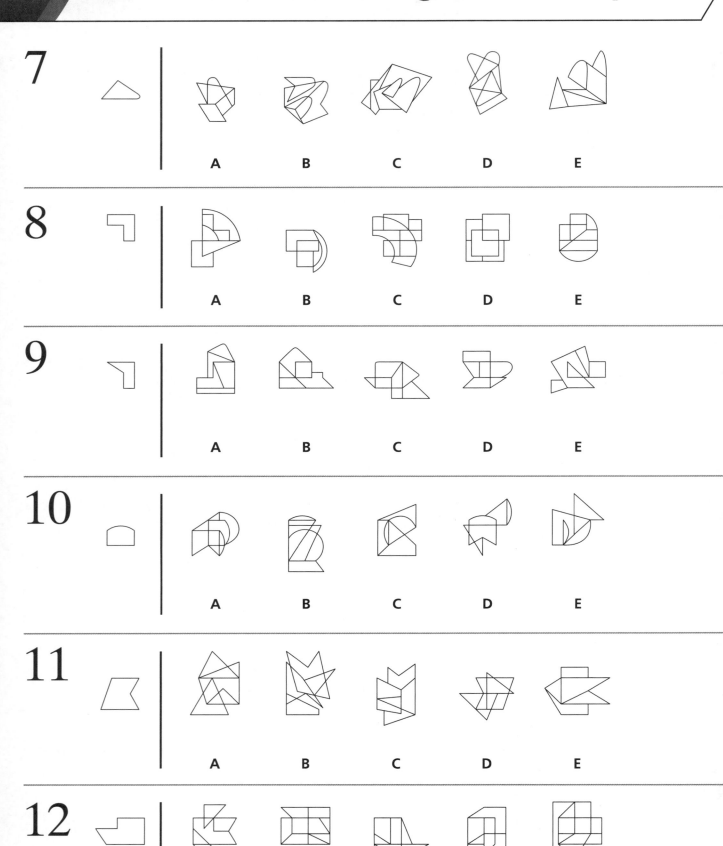

7

A   B   C   D   E

8

A   B   C   D   E

9

A   B   C   D   E

10

A   B   C   D   E

11

A   B   C   D   E

12

A   B   C   D   E

Section 4

Work out what makes the two figures on the left similar to each other. Then find the figure on the right that is **most like** the two figures on the left.

Example

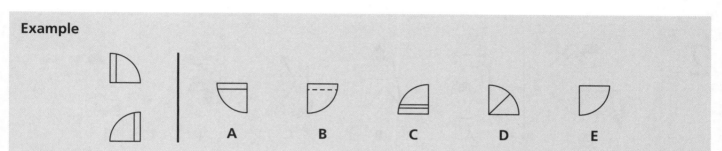

The two figures on the left-hand side are both made up of a quarter circle with a single solid line in alignment with one of the straight sides. The option most like these two figures is **A**. This has been marked on your answer sheet.

Now do the two practice questions below.

P1

The two figures on the left-hand side are both made up of a hairpin shape, with black 'feet' at the two straight ends and an arrow on the longer leg pointing outward. Therefore, the correct answer must be **D**, as it is the only figure which has these features. Mark the answer **D** in Practice Question 1 for Section 4 on your answer sheet.

P2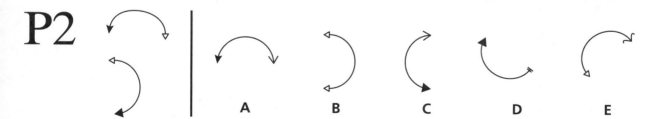

The two figures on the left-hand side both have one white triangular arrowhead and one mismatched arrowhead. Therefore, the correct answer must be **E**, as it is the only figure which has both these arrowheads. Mark the answer **E** in Practice Question 2 for Section 4 on your answer sheet.

Non-Verbal Reasoning Practice Paper

1

        A   **B**   **C**   **D**   **E**

2

        A   **B**   **C**   **D**   **E**

3

        A   **B**   **C**   **D**   **E**

4

        A   **B**   **C**   **D**   **E**

5

        A   **B**   **C**   **D**   **E**

6

        A   **B**   **C**   **D**   **E**

7

 |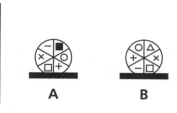

A   B   C   D   E

8

 |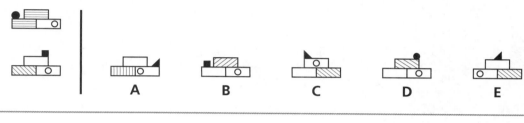

A   B   C   D   E

9

 |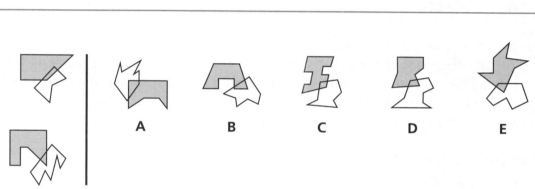

A   B   C   D   E

10

 |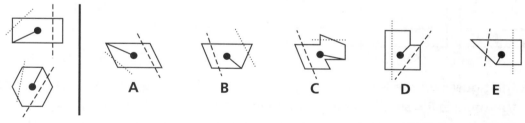

A   B   C   D   E

11

 |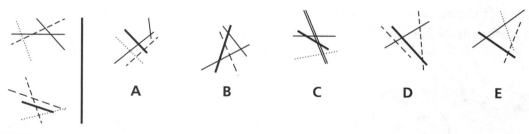

A   B   C   D   E

12

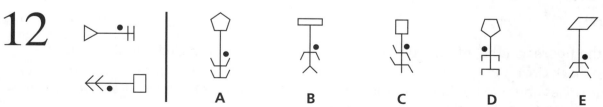

A   B   C   D   E

Non-Verbal Reasoning Practice Paper

Section 5

The figures on the left each have a code. Work out how the codes go with these figures. Then look at the image to the right of the vertical line and find its code from the five options given.

Example

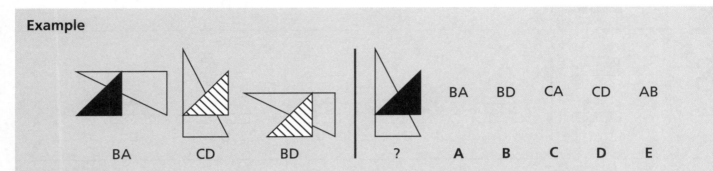

BA   CD   BD   ?   A   B   C   D   E

BA   BD   CA   CD   AB

In the figures on the left: B = large triangle has the right angle in the top right; C = large triangle has the right angle in the bottom left; A = small triangle is shaded black; D = small triangle is shaded with diagonal lines. The figure to the right has a large triangle with the right angle in the bottom left and the small triangle is shaded black. Therefore, the code is CA (option **C**). The correct answer is **C** and this has been marked on your answer sheet.

Now do the two practice questions below.

P1

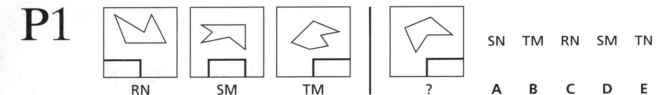

RN   SM   TM   ?   A   B   C   D   E

SN   TM   RN   SM   TN

In the figures on the left: M = irregular hexagon in the square; N = irregular pentagon in the square; R = small rectangle aligned to the left in the square; S = small rectangle aligned to the middle in the square; T = small rectangle aligned to the right in the square. The figure to the right has an irregular pentagon and the small rectangle is aligned to the right of the square. Therefore, the code is TN (option **E**). Mark the answer **E** in Practice Question 1 for Section 5 on your answer sheet.

P2

 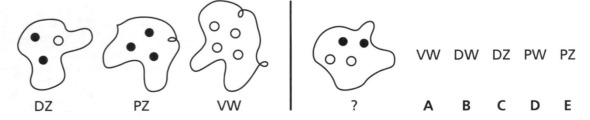

DZ   PZ   VW   ?   A   B   C   D   E

VW   DW   DZ   PW   PZ

In the figures on the left: Z = three circles in the loop; W = four circles in the loop; D = two black circles; P = three black circles; V = no black circles. The figure to the right has four circles and two are black, so the code is DW (option **B**). Mark the answer **B** in Practice Question 2 for Section 5 on your answer sheet.

You now have 6 minutes to complete the next 12 questions.

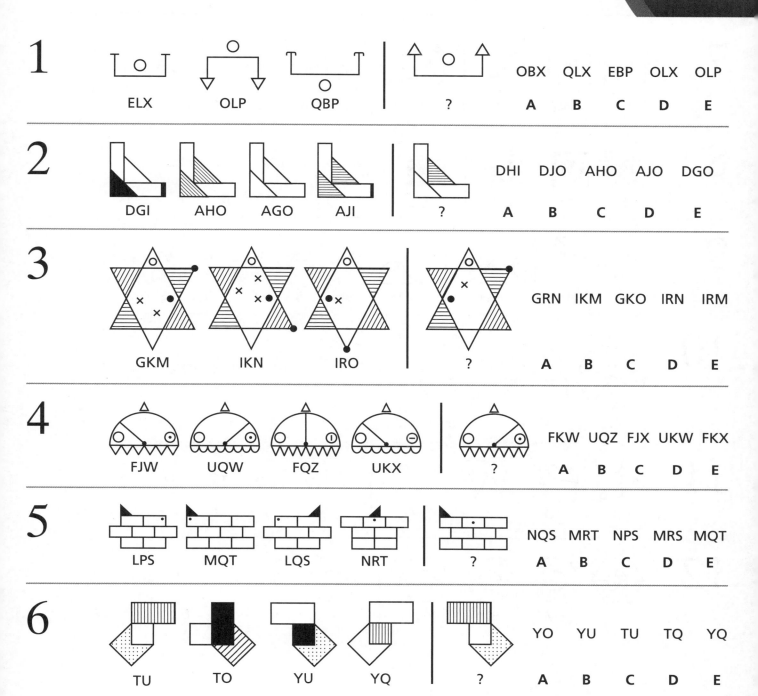

1

ELX   OLP   QBP   ?

OBX   QLX   EBP   OLX   OLP
  A   B   C   D   E

2

DGI   AHO   AGO   AJI   ?

DHI   DJO   AHO   AJO   DGO
 A   B   C   D   E

3

GKM   IKN   IRO   ?

GRN   IKM   GKO   IRN   IRM
 A   B   C   D   E

4

FJW   UQW   FQZ   UKX   ?

FKW   UQZ   FJX   UKW   FKX
 A   B   C   D   E

5

LPS   MQT   LQS   NRT   ?

NQS   MRT   NPS   MRS   MQT
 A   B   C   D   E

6

TU   TO   YU   YQ   ?

YO   YU   TU   TQ   YQ
 A   B   C   D   E

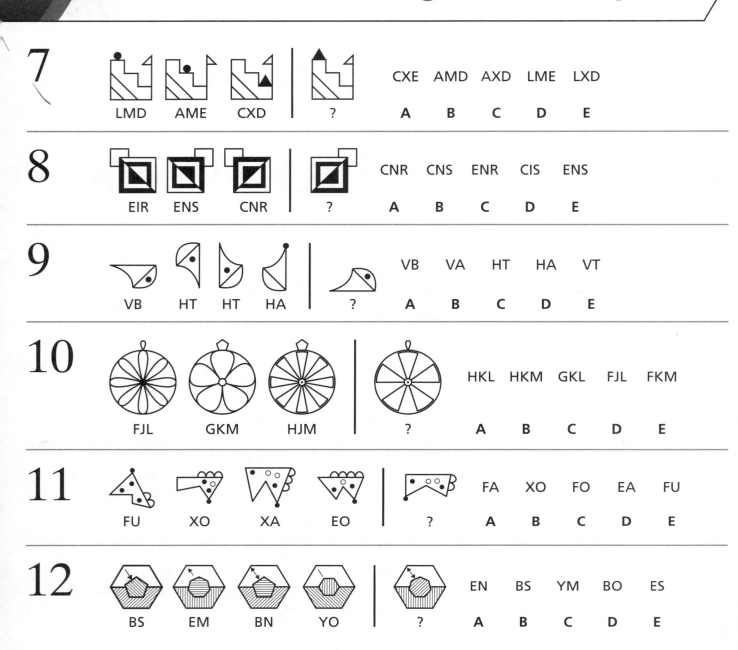

7

LMD	AME	CXD	?	CXE	AMD	AXD	LME	LXD
				A	**B**	**C**	**D**	**E**

8

EIR	ENS	CNR	?	CNR	CNS	ENR	CIS	ENS
				A	**B**	**C**	**D**	**E**

9

VB	HT	HT	HA	?	VB	VA	HT	HA	VT
					A	**B**	**C**	**D**	**E**

10

FJL	GKM	HJM	?	HKL	HKM	GKL	FJL	FKM
				A	**B**	**C**	**D**	**E**

11

FU	XO	XA	EO	?	FA	XO	FO	EA	FU
					A	**B**	**C**	**D**	**E**

12

BS	EM	BN	YO	?	EN	BS	YM	BO	ES
					A	**B**	**C**	**D**	**E**

END OF PAPER

Answers

Award 1 mark per correct answer unless otherwise stated.

Mathematics Activities

Pages 10–11
Challenge 1
a) 4   b) 4   c) 2   d) 5   e) 6   f) 2
Challenge 2
a) 4   b) 4   c) 5   d) 2   e) 7   f) 5
Challenge 3
a) 7.7   b) 5.94   c) 0.18   d) 2.83   e) 22.46
Challenge 4
a) 466.75   b) 467   c) 1,812.50   d) 484.624
e) 28.54204   f) 0.000312
Now Try This!
1. C
   Multiplying by 0.01 means moving the decimal point two places to the left. Therefore 46,892.4987 becomes 468.924987
2. a) A
   Work out the decimal point movements overall. 38.7 = one to the right, 2.462 = one to the left, so no movement and answer remains the same at 95.2794
   b) E
   387 = two to the right, 0.2462 = two to the left. So again the same answer at 95.2794

Pages 12–13
Challenge 1
a) 107   b) 239   c) 174   d) 4,537
e) 1,141   f) 15,611   g) 194   h) 5,496
Challenge 2
a) 221   b) 15   c) 12,413.50   d) 19
e) 11,424   f) 35   g) 2,152.2   h) 112.5
Challenge 3

17	×	9	=	153
589	+	492	=	1,081
99	÷	**9**	=	11
47	×	**0.01**	=	0.47
0.5	×	0.5	=	**0.25**
120	÷	0.25	=	480
105	÷	5	=	21
10,000	×	**0.0001**	=	1
0.594	×	**1,000**	=	594
0.5	÷	**2**	=	0.25

Challenge 4
a) 192 chairs
   12 × 16 = 192
b) 126 stickers
   226 − 28 − 72 = 126
c) £7.40
   First 20 minutes at 15p per minute = 20 × 0.15 = £3
   Next 22 minutes at 20p = 22 × 0.2 = £4.40
   £4.40 + £3 = £7.40

Now Try This!
1. B
   2,465 − 798 = 1,667
2. D
   Full price fares: 265 × £3.50 = £927.50
   Remainder of people = 483 − 265 = 218
   Half price fare = $\frac{£3.50}{2}$ = £1.75,
   £1.75 × 218 = £381.50
   Total spent = £927.50 + £381.50 = £1,309

Pages 14–15
Challenge 1

Fraction	Decimal	Percentage
$\frac{1}{2}$	0.5	50
$\frac{1}{4}$	0.25	**25**
$\frac{2}{5}$	**0.4**	40
$\frac{1}{5}$	0.2	**20**
$\frac{1}{10}$	**0.1**	10
$\frac{9}{20}$	0.45	**45**
$\frac{7}{25}$	**0.28**	**28**
$\frac{11}{50}$	**0.22**	22

Challenge 2
a) 0.06   b) $\frac{4}{5}$ c) 40%   d) 62.5%
e) $\frac{3}{20}$ f) $\frac{3}{10}$ g) 100%

Challenge 3
a) $\frac{1}{3}$
   $\frac{5}{15}$ simplified to $\frac{1}{3}$
b) 60%
   $\frac{3}{5}$ so $\frac{60}{100}$ = 60%

Challenge 4
a) 12 circles shaded
   20 circles so shade in 20 × 0.6 = 12
b) 6 circles shaded
   15 circles so shade in 15 × 0.4 = 6
Now Try This!
1. C
   Work out $\frac{2}{5}$ of 4,500: $\frac{4,500}{5}$ = 900,
   900 × 2 = 1,800
   Not wearing a hat = 4,500 − 1,800 = 2,700
   2,700 × 0.35 = 945

2. D
   We know that 33 marks = 55%
   So $\frac{33}{x}$ = $\frac{55}{100}$, $\frac{3,300}{x}$ = 55, x = 60.
   Rohit got 65% so 60 × 0.65 = 39.
   Rohit got 6 more marks than Sonia.

Pages 16–17
Challenge 1
a) 3 : 1   b) 5 : 4   c) £6   d) 4 : 2 : 1
Challenge 2
a) 55
   The ratio is 5 : 1. Add the ratios to get 6.
   $\frac{66}{6}$ = 11, 11 × Stan's ratio of 5 = 55
b) £40
   The ratio is 5 : 4. Add the ratios to get 9.
   $\frac{90}{9}$ = 10, 10 × Clara's ratio of 4 = £40
c) 36
   The ratio is 4 : 3. Add the ratios to get 7.
   $\frac{63}{7}$ = 9. 9 × boys' ratio of 4 = 36

Challenge 3

Boys	Girls	Ratio
10	12	5 : 6
6	12	**1 : 2**
14	20	**7 : 10**
6	**15**	2 : 5
28	**16**	7 : 4

Challenge 4
a) 6 : 2 : 1
b) £90
   The ratio is 6 : 3 : 1. Add the ratios to get 10.
   $\frac{300}{10}$ = 30, 30 × Carole's ratio of 3 = £90
c) £24
   The ratio is 8 : 4 : 1. Add the ratios to get 13.
   $\frac{312}{13}$ = 24, 24 × Phil's ratio of 1 = £24
d) 14
   Ratio = 0.5 : 1 : 3. Add the ratios to get 4.5
   $\frac{63}{4.5}$ = 14, 14 × Ranjeet's ratio of 1 = 14

Now Try This!
1. C
   A quarter of 160 = $\frac{160}{4}$ = 40
   Of the 120 left, ratio is 2 : 1. Add the ratios to get 3.
   $\frac{120}{3}$ = 40, 40 × two teams exactly ratio of 2 = 80
2. B
   The ratio is 5 : 1. Add the ratios to get 6.
   360 degrees in a pie chart so $\frac{360}{6}$ = 60
   60 × pants ratio of 1 = 60 degrees

Pages 18–19
Challenge 1
a) 20 cm
Perimeter = 5 cm × 4 equal sides of the square = 20 cm
b) 16 cm
Perimeter = (2 × 3 cm sides) + (2 × 5 cm sides) = 16 cm
c) 70 cm
Perimeter = 10 + 25 + 10 + 25 = 70 cm
Challenge 2
a) 81 cm² b) 88 cm² c) 24 cm²
Challenge 3

Width	Length	Perimeter	Area
15 cm	15 cm	**60 cm**	225 cm²
15 cm	20 cm	70 cm	**300 cm²**
20 cm	**10 cm**	60 cm	200 cm²
100 cm	100 cm	400 cm	**10,000 cm²**

Challenge 4
a) 86 cm
Perimeter = 11 + 25 + 18 + 15 = 69 + the two unknown sides. Find the sides from the other lengths, so (18 – 11) = 7 and (25 – 15) = 10, so 69 + 7 + 10 = 86
b) 380 cm²
To find area, break down into two rectangles, so (11 × 10) = 110, (15 × 18) = 270, 270 + 110 = 380 cm²
Now Try This!
1. E
If square has a perimeter of 40 cm, then width = $\frac{40}{4}$ = 10 cm
So Donna's square = 20 cm × 20 cm = 400 cm²
2. A
Right-angled triangle, so area = $\frac{(8 \times 12)}{2}$ = 48 cm²

Pages 20–21
Challenge 1
a) 60 degrees
Equilateral triangle means all the angles are the same, so $\frac{180}{3}$ = 60 degrees
b) 88 degrees
180 degrees in a triangle, so 180 – 46 – 46 = 88 degrees
c) Isosceles
Two angles are the same size, so it is an isosceles triangle.
Challenge 2
a) 52 degrees
180 degrees on a straight line, so the missing bottom right angle of the triangle is:
180 – 62 – 50 = 68 degrees
So angle x is:
180 – 60 – 68 = 52 degrees
b) 180 degrees
Cutting the square in half makes two triangles, so 180 degrees.

Challenge 3
a)
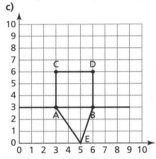
b) (5, 8)
Translating by (2, 2) means moving 2 right and 2 up so (5, 8).
c)
d) (5, 6)
Challenge 4
a) Square-based pyramid
b) Cone
Now Try This!
1. C
Isosceles triangle has two identical angles, so if 80 is the biggest then the other two must be $\frac{100}{2}$ = 50 degrees
2. B
Paula: radius 25 cm, diameter 50 cm
Jack: radius 50 cm, diameter 100 cm
Dave: radius 100 cm, diameter = 200 cm

Pages 22–23
Challenge 1
a) $y = 13$ b) $x = 4$ c) $x = 7$
d) $y = 5$ e) $y = 10$ f) $x = 15$
Challenge 2
a) $y = 22$
$7x + y = 85$, $(7 \times 9) + y = 85$, $63 + y = 85$
$y = 85 – 63$, $y = 22$
b) $y = 45$
$20x = 2y + 90$, $(20 \times 9) = 2y + 90$, $180 = 2y + 90$
$90 = 2y$, $y = 45$
c) $x = 50$
$(8 \times 12) + 4 = 50 + x$, $100 = 50 + x$, $x = 50$
d) $x = 2$
$(7 + 12) – x = 1$, $19 – x = 1$, $x = 18$
e) $y = 2$
$(2 \times –4) = –10 + y$, $–8 = –10 + y$, $y = 2$
f) $y = –5$
$–15 – –4 = –16 – y$, $–15 + 4 = –16 – y$, $–11 = –16 – y$, $5 = –y$, $y = –5$
Challenge 3
a) $x = 6$
$17x – 22 = 5x + 50$, $17x – 5x = 50 + 22$
$12x = 72$, $x = 6$
b) $y = 2$
$14y^2 = 56$, $14(y^2) = 56$
So $y^2 = 4$, $y = 2$
c) $x = 5$
$\frac{50}{x} = 2x$, $50 = 2x^2$, $x = 5$

d) $y = 1$
$20y^2 = 20$, $y = 1$
Challenge 4
a) $y = 5$
$3 + 2x(y + 1) = 27$, $3 + 4(y + 1) = 27$, $3 + 4y + 4 = 27$
$4y = 20$, $y = 5$
b) $y = 1$
$29 + 3x(y + 7) = 77$, $29 + 6(y + 7) = 77$, $29 + 6y + 42 = 77$
$6y = 6$, $y = 1$
c) $y = 3$
$(16 \times 9) + 16 + 9y = 190 – y$, $144 + 16 + 9y = 190 – y$, $160 + 9y = 190 – y$, $10y = 30$, $y = 3$
d) $y = 9$
$(9^2 + 25) + 2y = 133 – y$, $106 + 2y = 133 – y$, $3y = 27$, $y = 9$
Now Try This!
1. E
It is $4(4y + 2) = 16y + 8$
2. A
It is $2(3x + y) + 2(5x + 2y) = 6x + 2y + 10x + 4y = 16x + 6y$

Pages 24–25
Challenge 1
a) 20p
$3R + 2P = 1.90$, so $3(0.5) + 2P = 1.90$,
$1.5 + 2P = 1.90$
$2P = 0.4$, P = 20p
b) $3x + 2y = 9$
c) 50p
$4C + 3B = 6.50$, $4C + 3(1.5) = 6.5$, $4C + 4.50 = 6.5$, $4C = 2$, C = 50p
d) $14x = 7$
Challenge 2
a) $y = 8$
$4y + x = 38$, so $4y + 6 = 38$
$4y = 32$, $y = 8$
b) $y = 10$
$9y + 2x = 120$, so $9y + 2(15) = 120$,
$9y + 30 = 120$
$9y = 90$, $y = 10$
c) $y = 1$
$17y + 3(15) = 62$, $17y + 45 = 62$,
$17y = 17$, $y = 1$
d) $y = 60$
$300 – y – 3(50) = 90$, $300 – y – 150 = 90$, $150 – y = 90$, $y = 60$
Challenge 3
a) i) $6y + 16y = 5$
ii) $8x + 2y = 14.50$
b) i) $21y + 6x = 9$
ii) $3y + 27x = 42$
c) $4x = 2.50$
$(4y + 7x = 5.50) – (4y + 3x = 3.00)$ is
$4x = 2.50$
d) $8y + 4x = 18$
$(20y + 10x = 45) – (12y + 6x = 27)$ is
$8y + 4x = 18$
Challenge 4
a) $x = 1$, $y = 0.5$
Multiply second equation by 2 to get
$4x + 6y = 7$
Subtract first equation from that to get
$4y = 2$
So $4y = 2$, $y = 0.5$
Put into original equation to get
$4x + 2(0.5) = 5$
$4x = 4$, $x = 1$
So $x = 1$, $y = 0.5$

b) $x = 0.8, y = 1.25$
Double the first equation to get
$6x + 4y = 9.8$; subtract second equation
to get $2x = 1.60, x = 0.8$
Substitute into first equation to get
$3(0.8) + 2y = 4.90, 2.4 + 2y = 4.9,$
$2y = 2.5, y = 1.25$

c) $x = 1.05, y = 1.30$
Double second equation to get
$10x + 4y = 15.7$; subtract first equation
to get $7x = 7.35, x = 1.05$
Substitute into first equation to get
$3(1.05) + 4y = 8.35, 3.15 + 4y = 8.35,$
$4y = 5.2, y = 1.30$

Now Try This!

1. **D**
$3E + 5P = 3.80$
$6E + 4P = 5.20$
So double first equation to get
$6E + 10P = 7.60$
Subtract second equation to get
$6P = 2.40, P = 40p$
Put in original equation to get
$3E + 5(0.4) = 3.80, 3E = 1.80, E = 60p$
So 1 envelope = 60p, 1 pen = 40p

2. **B**
$4R + 3C = 4.10$
$3R + 6C = 5.70$
Double first equation to get
$8R + 6C = 8.20$
Subtract second equation to get
$5R = 2.50, R = 50p$
Put in first equation to get
$4(0.5) + 3C = 4.10, 2 + 3C = 4.10,$
$3C = 2.10, C = 70p$
So 1 kitchen roll = 50p, 1 cheese slice = 70p

Pages 26–27
Challenge 1
a) 12
$\text{Mean} = \frac{(8 + 11 + 8 + 16 + 17)}{5} = 12$
b) 8
Mode is the most common value, so 8.
c) 9
Range = 17 − 8 = 9
d) 11
Median is the middle value when
ordered to 8, 8, 11, 16, 17
e) 30
30 − 8 = 22

Challenge 2
a) 0
b) 11
$\text{Mean} = \frac{(9 + 0 + 0 + 24 + 12 + 21)}{6} = 11$
c) 10.5
Values when ordered are 0, 0, 9, 12, 21, 24
$\text{Median} = \frac{(9 + 12)}{2} = 10.5$
d) 24
24 − 0 = 24
e) 15
$9 + 0 + 0 + 48 + 12 + 21 = 90$
$\frac{90}{6} = 15$
f) 48
48 − 0 = 48
g) 10.5
Values when ordered are 0, 0, 9, 12, 21, 48
$\text{Median} = \frac{(9 + 12)}{2} = 10.5$

Challenge 3
a) 20
20 is the most common number of stickers.
b) 20
When ordered, the data values are 10, 15, 20, 20, 25
c) 15
25 − 10 = 15
d) 18
$\frac{(10 + 15 + 20 + 20 + 25)}{5} = 18$

Challenge 4
a) 7
10 − 3 = 7
b) 14
Mode = 3, median = 5, mean = 6
3 + 5 + 6 = 14

Now Try This!

1. **A**
After 7 results the mean will be 64.
That must mean her total marks
would have been 64 × 7 = 448.
So 448 − 64 − 58 − 66 − 49 − 58 − 74 = 79

2. **E**
If a, b, c have a mode of 15 then both b
and c must be 15. A mean of 13 means
the total of $a + b + c = 39$ as $\frac{39}{3} = 13$, so
39 − 15 − 15 = 9. Therefore $a + b = 9 + 15 = 24$

Pages 28–29
Challenge 1
a)

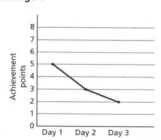

b) 10
5 + 3 + 2 = 10
c) 3
5 − 2 = 3

Challenge 2

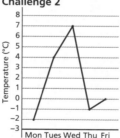

Challenge 3

Colour	Number	Size of pie chart angle
Red	25	90°
Blue	**50**	180°
Green	25	90°

Challenge 4
a) 24
The given percentages add up to 30 + 34 + 24 = 88, so netball must be 12%.
12% is half of 24% so $\frac{48}{2} = 24$

b) 200
If 48 = 24% then $\frac{48}{x} = \frac{24}{100}, \frac{4,800}{x} = 24,$
$x = 200$

Now Try This!
1. **C**
So $\frac{2}{5}$ are not looking at their phone. $\frac{1}{5}$
therefore looking out of the window.
$\frac{1}{5} \times 360 = 72$ degrees

2. **D**
240 : 120 = 2 : 1 ratio.
Add ratios to get 3. $\frac{360}{3} = 120$
120 × 2 = 240 degrees

Pages 30–33
1. **a)** 70
Prime factors of 10 = 2 × 5
Prime factors of 14 = 2 × 7
2 × 5 × 7 = 70
b) 2
Factors of 8 = 1, 2, 4, 8
Factors of 14 = 1, 2, 7, 14
So highest common factor is 2

2. **a)** 3 hours 8 minutes
14:28 to 17:36 = 3 hours 8 minutes
b) 20:37
41 minutes later than 19:56 is 20:37

3. **a)** Town B
b) 71 miles
c) 11 miles
Town B is 43 miles from Town A and
Town D is 54 miles from Town A.
54 − 43 = 11 miles

4. **a)** 33
Adding 6 each time.
b) 86
The two previous numbers are added.
c) 11
The first, third, fifth and therefore
seventh numbers increase by 3 each time.

5. **a)** (2, −2)
b) (−4, −3)

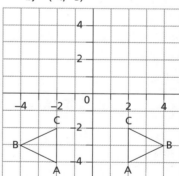

6. 5 km
10 km/hr = $\frac{10}{60}$ per minute = $\frac{1}{6}$ per minute.
$24 \times \frac{1}{6} = \frac{24}{6} = 4$ km
5 km/hr = $\frac{5}{60}$ per minute = $\frac{1}{12}$ per minute.
$12 \times \frac{1}{12} = 1$ km, so 4 + 1 = 5 km

7. **a)** 180 degrees
There are 60 minutes in an hour
and 360 degrees in a circle, so each
minute is $\frac{360}{60} = 6$ degrees. At 6:00
there will be 30 minutes between
the hands, so 180 degrees.

b) 75 degrees

At 3:30 the hour hand will be halfway between 3 and 4, so there will be 12.5 minutes between them. 12.5 × 6 = 75 degrees

8. a) (0, −1)

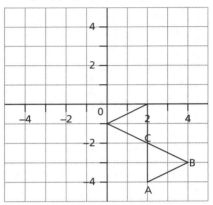

b) (−2, 2)

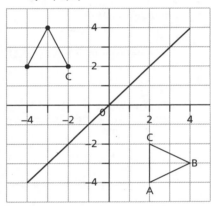

9. 1.25 miles

He is going for 15 minutes at 5 mph.

$\frac{15}{60} = 0.25$

0.25 × 5 = 1.25 miles

10. $\frac{1}{4}$

Probability of a head with one toss of the coin is $\frac{1}{2}$

$\frac{1}{2} \times \frac{1}{2} = \frac{1}{4}$

11. a) 50%

2, 4, 6, 8, 10, 12, 14, 16, 18, 20 = 10 numbers

$\frac{10}{20} = 50\%$

b) 30%

1, 2, 4, 5, 10, 20

$\frac{6}{20}$ so 30%

c) 20%

1, 4, 9, 16

$\frac{4}{20}$ so 20%

d) 40%

2, 3, 5, 7, 11, 13, 17, 19

$\frac{8}{20}$ so 40%

12. a) West

b) South East

English Activities

Pages 34–35

Challenge 1

a) Various answers are possible. Answers may include comments about the metaphor and alliteration in 'killed by kindness' which suggests that the family is warm and caring, or the simile 'like bees swarming after their queen', which suggests that the daughters follow their mother's lead in attending to Mr March. Overall, the atmosphere is considerate, loving and friendly.

b) Various answers are possible. Answers should focus on the last sentence of the extract in comparison with the first part. Initially, the passage explains that the mother and daughters abandon everything else to look after Mr March. The last sentence, contrastingly, suggests that the adults feel concerned and anxious when they look at Meg and implies that there is something amiss that preoccupies their previously happy thoughts.

[Award 1 mark for the selection of a suitable quotation and 2 marks for analysis of the effect of the quotation.]

Challenge 2

a) Various answers are possible. Answers could include:

- Comment about the slow pace of the lid of the cylinder being removed, creating suspense.
- Comment about the narrator nearly being pushed towards this mysterious object, creating tension.
- Comment about the language used to describe the light/shade in the last two sentences, creating mystery.

[The strongest candidates will use a P-E-A structure (a point made in their own words, followed by supporting evidence in the form of a quotation from the passage, then an analytical section explaining in greater detail). Each section of the PEA answer scores 1 mark (no marks for repetition of the evidence without the child's own words).]

b) Various answers are possible. Answers should suggest that it is something really unusual or unknowable as it does not have a name in English (otherwise it would not be a 'Thing'). The Thing could be an alien creature emerging from the cylinder, or refer to the cylinder itself (with justification).

[Up to 3 marks awarded for quality of the answer and justification of the selection.]

Challenge 3

a) Chosen words and phrases which suggest a mysterious, ominous atmosphere could include:

- 'Stranger' – someone unknown/mysterious.
- 'Driving snow' – bleak, cold setting which is uncomfortable for the characters.

- 'Wrapped up from head to foot' and 'hid every inch of his face' – we cannot see much of the narrator so he becomes more mysterious.
- 'More dead than alive' – creates tension/mystery as we do not know why he is in this state.

[Award up to 3 marks.]

b) Overall, the setting is ominous, spooky and bleak. Answers could make reference to the overall negative atmosphere created through the use of unpleasant imagery, a mysterious character and pathetic fallacy in the form of the snowfall.

[Award up to 2 marks.]

Challenge 4

a) Suggestions for various atmospheres that could be created are: mysterious; chaotic; oppressive; melancholy; stilted

[Award 1 mark per suggestion]

b) Give credit in the story for a sophisticated range of syntax and an awareness of how description can shape an atmosphere. Award marks for accuracy of spelling, punctuation and grammar and originality of plot. Any resemblance to well-known stories such as *Harry Potter* should not be accepted.

[Award up to 10 marks for content, plot and characterisation and up to 5 marks for the spelling, punctuation and grammar.]

Now Try This!

C There is much scandal as it is a tantalising story

We are told that there is 'intense interest' and the case is notorious. There are 'sensational rumours', which indicates that people are still interested in what had happened.

Pages 36–37

Challenge 1

Possible answers include:

a) The poem's title emphasises the listeners, rather than the traveller himself.

b) The Traveller's name is withheld because the 'phantom listeners' are almost more significant than he is. We are drawn to the Traveller's confusion when he is 'perplexed and still' and share his disconcerted response to the silent, ominous presence of the strange ghostly spirits. *[3 marks]*

c) He feels confused and cannot believe that the house is deserted *[1 mark]*. The Traveller was clearly expecting someone to be in, as he has some clear reason to be at the house and knocked a second time to be certain no one would answer. *[1 mark]*

d) i) Ghostly occupants of the house ('phantom listeners') who are not the Traveller's intended audience. *[2 marks]*

ii) The Traveller senses the phantoms' presence ('And he felt in his heart their strangeness') *[1 mark]*. He seems to communicate with the listeners and have an understanding with them despite them not replying to him ('Their stillness answering his cry') [1 mark]. He speaks to the spirits with an instruction. [1 mark]

e) i) 'Tell them that I came, and no one answered, / That I kept my word.'

ii) The Traveller is a man with high morals who does not go back on his word. When he comes to the door, we learn that he has a prior arrangement and has kept his promise to be there ('I kept my word'). He speaks confidently, with his head 'lifted' and knocks 'loudly'.

f) Alliteration ('forest's ferny floor'); sensory description ('sound of iron on stone' or 'listening in the quiet of the moonlight'); rhetorical question ('Is there anybody there?'); repetition ('Is there anybody there?' or 'smote on the door'). Analysis will vary but could include explanation about vivid imagery created for the reader, creation of suspense or tension.
[3 marks for a detailed, comprehensive answer for each technique]

Challenge 2
Answers will vary.
[1 mark per mind map]

Challenge 3
Answers will vary. Give credit for originality.
[Award up to 6 marks for a well-rounded answer that considers each aspect suggested]

Now Try This!
D Creative and indolent
Rocky must be creative because he writes poetry for a living. He is also extremely lazy as he works the fewest number of days he can each year, and rests afterwards.

Pages 38–39
Challenge 1
Answers will vary, but could include:
- Mr Tulliver is not well-educated himself and is not an articulate man ('more schoolin' nor I ever got').
- He is determined that his son will receive more education than he did and this will help with the family business ('these lawsuits, and arbitrations, and things').
- Mr Tulliver does not have a high opinion of the legal profession ('I wouldn't make a downright lawyer o' the lad, – I should be sorry for him to be a raskill').
- Mr Tulliver is ambitious for Tom.
[Award up to 6 marks. The strongest candidates will use a P-E-A structure (a _point_ made in their own words, followed by supporting _evidence_ in the form of a quotation from the passage, then an _analytical_ section explaining in greater detail). Each section of the PEA answer scores 1 mark (no marks for repetition of the evidence without the child's own words).]

Challenge 2
a) She is determined, outgoing and confident. Pollyanna seems to act rashly, without fully considering a plan before jumping in and getting started. She does not seem to think about consequences. Pollyanna is spontaneous, impulsive and astute, and notices her surroundings in great detail.
[Award up to 3 marks, 1 per detail]

b) Given what we know of Pollyanna in the story, it is likely she will make her way to the rock and stand on top. She will likely do this at great speed and with athleticism. We know this because she clings 'like a monkey' to the tree when climbing down it and in the last line, she feels like there is 'just one place in the world worth being in – the top of that big rock'.
[Award up to 3 marks. 1 mark for a suitable quotation; 2 marks for the analysis]

Challenge 3
Answers should have a sophisticated range of syntax and an awareness of how description can shape an atmosphere. Award marks for accuracy of spelling, punctuation and grammar and originality of plot. Any resemblance to well-known stories such as _Harry Potter_ should not be accepted.
[Award up to 10 marks for content, plot and characterisation and up to 5 marks for the spelling, punctuation and grammar.]

Now Try This!
B He is elusive and mysterious
Basil Hallward is shown in the extract to be wondering where Dorian might have got to the previous evening and felt a 'miserable' at not finding Dorian.

Pages 40–41
Challenge 1
a) receipt   b) eight   c) yield
d) fierce   e) beige

Challenge 2

Words spelt ei after 'c' with an 'ee' sound	Words spelt ei with an 'ee', 'ay', 'ih' or an 'i' sound	Words spelt ie with an 'ee' sound	Exceptions
receipt deceit	protein eight forfeit height	field believe	glacier science ancient

Challenge 3
The following words should be underlined:
oases; axes; appendices; dice; media; larvae

Challenge 4
a) geese   b) trout   c) diagnoses
d) ellipses   e) quizzes   f) series
g) leaves   h) oxen   i) aircraft

Now Try This!
1. C
The word should be spelt 'receive'.
2. A
The word should be spelt 'shrieked'.
3. D
The word should be spelt 'deer'.

4. D
The word should be spelt 'vertices'.

Pages 42–43
Challenge 1
a) impractical   b) misinform
c) indefinite   d) decompose
e) uneven   f) irrespective
g) distrust (or mistrust)   h) illegal
i) inactive

Challenge 2
Any suitable answers, such as:
a) semi – half   b) mono – single
c) uni – everyone   d) sub – below
e) auto – self   f) super – bigger or better than usual
g) tele – far away   h) bi – two

Challenge 3
a) i) malicious   ii) repetitious
iii) spacious   iv) infectious
b) i) confidential   ii) essential
iii) facial   iv) presidential

Challenge 4
a) i) alliance   ii) difference
iii) insurance   iv) tolerance
v) adherence   vi) obedience
b) i) preference, preferring, preferred
ii) inference, inferring, inferred

Now Try This!
1. C
The word should be spelt 'referee'.
2. B
The word should be spelt 'impartial'.
3. A
The word should be spelt 'fictitious'.
4. B
The word should be spelt 'hesitancy'.

Pages 44–45
Challenge 1
a) pneumonia   b) silhouette
c) psychology   d) rhombus
e) doubtful   f) vehicle
g) pterodactyl   h) knead

Challenge 2
a) solemn   b) parliament
c) receipt   d) succumb
e) government

Challenge 3
a) The following words should be circled:
i) reign   ii) alter   iii) bare
iv) dissent   v) practise
b) i) edition   ii) precede
iii) except   iv) cease
v) excess   vi) dessert

Challenge 4
The correct spellings are:
due; weather; so; proceeded; alternative; There; guest; which; knew; reasonably; priced; great; were; quite; weary; finally; scenery; spectacular; beach; There; preferred; dams [½ mark for each correct answer]

Now Try This!
1. C
The word should be spelt 'wandering'.
2. B
The word should be spelt 'advice'.
3. N
There is no mistake.

Pages 46–47

Challenge 1

a) i) How shocking the weather was on Monday!

ii) Neil Armstrong was an American astronaut and the first man on the Moon.

b) What is the best novel you've ever read ✓

Challenge 2

a) i) If you turn right at the end of the road, you'll see the church, the car park and the cemetery on the left-hand side.

ii) Before we ate, Freda, Malachy, Klaus and Nav insisted on going for some fresh air.

b) The comma indicates that Finlay asked three people (Stanley, Morgan and Jamie) to come for a sleepover. In the first sentence, there are only two people (Stanley Morgan and Jamie).

Challenge 3

a) "I'd give anything to be lying on a beach," sighed Maggie. "I'm so fed up."

b) "There's no point in moaning," said Archie, "because you know Dad said we can't go this year."

c) "Well, the last thing I want to do is go camping again, Archie. It'll be cold, wet and boring."

d) "How do you know? Do you have a crystal ball?" Archie demanded, crossly.

Challenge 4

Matthew has just read an article about

D T   I

Ðr ¢hompson. İt seems that he likes

a cup of hot chocolate at bedtime,

           O

a piece of toast and a biscuit. Øne of his

         H

colleagues revealed: "Ħe is firm but fair.

I

İn the summer time he loves going camping

          H

with his wife and children. Ħe particularly

   W   C   M   A

likes ᵥⱳarwick ¢astle, ᵯmalmesbury ᵃabbey and

B   P   C

Ƀlenheim ᵖpalace in the ¢otswolds.

Now Try This!

1. **B** at his watch,
A comma is needed after a fronted adverbial.

2. **N**
There is no mistake.

3. **C** "I've got this," he said
The closing inverted commas should come *after* the comma.

4. **C** mental determination, he
There should be a comma after a fronted adverbial.

Pages 48–49

Challenge 1

Sentence	Contraction	Possession
There've been lots of robberies in our local area recently.	✓	
Celia's friends are coming round to celebrate her birthday.		✓
I could have sworn you're related to my next-door neighbour.	✓	
You really will be shocked when you see Mum's new haircut.		✓

Challenge 2

a) i) should've   ii) they'd

iii) shan't   iv) I'd

v) won't   vi) couldn't've

b) i) the prince's crown

ii) those princes' crowns

iii) the fox's cubs

iv) the foxes' dens

v) the children's ski school

vi) the men's changing rooms

Challenge 3

Cautiously, the lion nudges its young cubs and pushes them along the savannah. **It's** cooler now as the sun is starting to lose its intense heat as it starts its descent below the horizon. The youngest cub tries to catch up with its family but **it's** hard to match their eager pace. Soon, they find themselves on the edge of the jungle; **it's** a riot of noise but **it's** not long before they find a quiet clearing in which to bed down for the night.

Challenge 4

The recent unpredictable **weather's** playing havoc with **Dad's** vegetables. **He's** been out there from the crack of dawn for weeks, digging and planting, though admittedly **Mum's** helped him from time to time. **He's** had the usual trouble with caterpillars and slugs as well, but even he **wasn't** expecting the extent to which **they've** eaten through his cabbages and lettuces. **We're** normally tucking into home-grown tomatoes and cucumber at this time of year but it **isn't** looking like **they'll** be adorning our plates any time soon. Luckily, the local **farmers'** vegetables have not been affected so I think **we'll** be paying them a visit.

Now Try This!

1. **A** Amie's
The apostrophe is needed to replace the 'i' in 'is'.

2. **D** women's
The apostrophe comes after the irregular plural noun 'women' and before the 's'.

3. **A** we're
The apostrophe is needed to replace the 'a' in 'are'.

Pages 50–51

Challenge 1

a) My mum is a famous author and poet – you'll definitely have heard of her.

b) Without a doubt, Millie's resilience – not to mention her extreme courage – saw her through the awful ordeal.

c) Our trek through the Amazon rainforest – incredible as it was – left me feeling weak and exhausted.

Challenge 2

a) This week we are covering the following in maths: area, perimeter and volume.

b) Erin's been visiting Scotland for years; she loves the scenery and the people.

c) The judge in the murder trial announced his verdict – guilty.

Challenge 3

a) I'd really love to visit the following places: the wild national parks on the island of Hokkaido, Japan; the Grotta Azzurra on the island of Capri, Italy; Recoleta and La Boca, Buenos Aries; and the Niagara Falls in Ontario, Canada.

b) After the performance, Mr McGrath – our drama teacher – made his final announcement: "Please take care as the car park will be busy." We all filed outside (it was dark already) and searched for our parents' cars. It had been a great show – an experience I'll never forget.
[Accept the pair of dashes in place of the brackets and vice versa]

Challenge 4

a) The surgeon (with her usual dexterity) performed the life-saving operation to the relief of all.

b) We'd intended to take the early train – the show was a matinee – but unfortunately it was cancelled.

c) Our school caretaker, who's an avid reader and researcher, is appearing on *Mastermind* this week.

d) Gustav and Mo admired (but didn't buy) the painting on display.
[For a), c) and d), accept brackets, dashes or commas; for b) accept dashes or brackets]

Now Try This!

1. **C** and exotic fruits – everything
A dash or a colon is required after 'fruits' to introduce the clause giving more detail to the first.

2. **A** for. Hugo – always the
An initial dash is required before the start of the parenthetic phrase 'always the first to do anything'.

3. **D** of the waterfall; carefully, she
A semi-colon is required to link the two closely related clauses.

4. **N**
There is no mistake.

Pages 52–53

Challenge 1

a) A few years ago, we <u>decide</u> to <u>go</u> camping. It <u>was</u> our first time and I <u>must</u> say, we <u>were</u> very excited. Little <u>do</u> we <u>know</u> that it <u>is</u> going to <u>rain</u> the entire time! However, I <u>wouldn't</u> <u>say</u> it <u>ruins</u> our trip – we <u>are able</u> to <u>spend</u> the evenings in the recreation room where we <u>play</u> table tennis and <u>meet</u> lots of new friends.

b) A few years ago, we **decided** to go camping. It was our first time and I must say, we were very excited. Little **did** we know that it **was** going to rain the entire time! However, I wouldn't say it **ruined** our trip – we **were** able to spend the evenings in the recreation room where we **played** table tennis and **met** lots of new friends.

Challenge 2
a) We **saw those/the/these** same street musicians when we went shopping last week.
b) Salena said she would **have taken** her little brother to the park if she'd been asked.

Challenge 3
The following words should be underlined:
a) Rick
b) you
c) The amazing acrobats   (also accept 'the acrobats')
d) Buckingham Palace

Challenge 4
a) A group of Year 6 children **is/was** representing the school at the debate.
b) Mum said my sister and I **are/were** allowed to go into town on our bikes.
c) If I **were** to win a million pounds, I'd cruise around the Caribbean.
d) Should you **be** cold, please turn on the heating.

Now Try This!
1. C   those
The demonstrative determiner 'those' modifies 'long-ago school days'.
2. E   filled up
Simple past tense agreeing with 'my eyes'.
3. D   had been
Past perfect tense agreeing with the plural pronoun 'we'.
4. A   as
The adverb 'as', forming the adverbial phrase 'as young children'

Pages 54–59
1. C
Mrs Hay is made to seem kind for sending the present.
2. E
The house is not perfect as the paint has drips and is 'oily', but it is made to seem exciting despite this.
3. A
We read that the door is stuck, creating suspense before the description of how it opens and we see the interior all at once.
4. D
We are told the lamp does not really work and the red chairs are in the drawing room.
5. C
The Burnells are described as looking down on everyone else in the village.
6. A
Isabel whips the other girls into a frenzy by creating suspense.
7. D
Isabel enjoys being the centre of attention whilst explaining about the doll's house.
8. E
The Kelvey girls are unkindly left out as they are considered to be socially inferior to the other children.

9. E
hyperbole
10. C
fenceposts
11. C
personification
12. E
assemble
13. E
conjunction
14. C
determiner
15. D
pronoun
16. a) analyses   b) tuna
    c) data   d) swine
    e) series   f) crises
17. "It's time to walk to the train station," said Frances. "We don't want to miss the 7:05."
"Isn't there a later train we can get?" asked Doug. "If we're there too early, we'll only be hanging around."
"Better safe than sorry," replied Doug's sister, Emilie. "It's too important. We can't afford to be late."
(also accept: a semi-colon instead of a full stop after 'important'; an exclamation mark instead of a full stop after 'the 7:05', 'hanging around', 'sorry', 'important' and 'late')
18. a) Charlie and Philippa have gone on holiday but they come back tomorrow.
(also accept: 'they will come back' or 'they will be coming back')
    b) Before we started our test, our teacher told us to check each answer carefully.
(also accept: 'we start' and 'our teacher tells')
    c) "When were you going to tell me that you wouldn't be able to come to my party?"
(also accept: "When are you going to tell me that you aren't able to come to my party?")
19. a) inactive   b) illiterate
    c) impenetrable   d) disrespect
20.

Nouns	Adjectives
residence	residential
preference	preferable /
vacation / vacancy	preferred
application / appliance	vacant
consideration	applicable
reliance	considerable /
	considerate
	reliable

21. a) believe; chief; deceitful
    b) language; fluency; strangely
    c) cashier; caffeine-free; receipt
    d) presidential; allowed; significant
22. a) spacious / spatial   b) fictitious
    c) beneficial   d) repetitious
    e) malicious   f) palatial
23. a) twelfth   b) obedience   c) intensify

Verbal Reasoning Activities

Pages 60–61
Challenge 1
a) fundamentalist: fund, dame, list (also: amen)
   restaurant: rest, aura, rant
   motherboard: moth, herb, boar
b) dine; died; hind; hide
Challenge 2
a) 5th and 6th letter of first word, followed by 3rd letter of first word.
b) 3rd and 4th letter of first word, followed by 'e' then 1st letter of first word.
c) First four letters are reversed to form 2nd word.
Challenge 3
a) With practice, Ja**mes h**ad the potential to be a gr**eat s**inger.
   mesh, eats (also accept: alto)
b) Use of **lea**d-based paints proved the cause of t**he art**ist's death.
   flea, hear
c) A musi**cal m**edley comprising a range of **act**s received great reviews.
   calm, fact
d) The loc**k nee**ds to be fixed by a locksmith thi**s inst**ance.
   knee, sins
Challenge 4
a) My ca**t cap**tured a rodent in the back garden.
   pact
b) Harry exceeds **in ever**ything he ever does!
   even
c) Last night, we had our pian**o reh**earsal.
   hero
d) The vet said she mu**st op**erate on Monty immediately.
   pots
Now Try This!
1. a) bu**t our**   tour
   b) anot**her d**ownside   herd
2. a) best
   1st, 5th, 6th, 7th letters
   b) done
   4th, 2nd, 3rd, 5th letters

Pages 62–63
Challenge 1
a) sea, ear, arc
b) can, did, ate (also: and)
c) for, mid, dab
d) car, pen, try
e) rot, the, her
f) hot, the, her, era, rap
Challenge 2
a) WONDERED   b) NEWSPAPER
c) CRIMINAL   d) FUNCTIONAL
e) LICENCE   f) NEGOTIATE
g) CHIMNEY   h) SLAPSTICK
Challenge 3
a) rare
b) leaf
c) mash
Challenge 4
a) eat   ate
b) fan   fun
c) pit   pet
d) mat   met

Now Try This!
1. a) MEN   b) PER
2. a) lad
   3rd and 2nd letter from 1st word, followed by 1st letter of 2nd word.
   b) skin
   4th letter from 2nd word, 5th letter from 1st word, 3rd letter from 2nd word, then 4th letter from 1st word.
   c) rare
   Take letters 2 and 4 from the 2nd word and add the 2nd and 3rd letters from the first word.

Pages 64–65
Challenge 1
BOYS
SHE
ANGER
AT
STARED
SILLY
THE
IN
SHE STARED IN ANGER AT THE SILLY BOYS.
Challenge 2

Word pairs		New word pairs	Letter you moved
stand	sable	sand stable	t
trend	tough	tend trough	r
chart	hump	hart chump	c
hone	sank	one shank	h
cream	wan	cram wane	e
slope	port	lope sport	s
twine	lean	wine leant	t

The seven-letter word is **stretch**.
Challenge 3
Answers will vary. Examples:
a) i) button, sew
   ii) chill, care
b) i) isle
   ii) pare/pair
   iii) quay
   iv) berth
Challenge 4
a) debit   b) secrete   c) gripped
d) freight   e) thread   f) soldier
Now Try This!
1. a) T (ROLL / COMPLAINT)
   b) I (SAVOUR / PAINT)
   c) U (ROTE / BUOY)
2. a) B   pelt
   b) D   faint

Pages 66–67
Challenge 1
Answers will vary. Examples:
bark: The noise a dog makes (N) / To make a loud, rough noise (V) / The rough outer covering on a tree (N)
address: The place where someone lives/works (N) / A formal speech (N) / To speak to someone (V)
stem: The part of the plant that grows above ground (N) / The thin part of a glass that attaches to the base (N) / To stop something from increasing (V)

Challenge 2

Verb	Noun	Can be both a verb and a noun
itemise	candle	blow
breathe	desk	glare
devastate	reporter	level

Challenge 3
a) As the troops <u>approached</u> the besieged city, the panicked inhabitants <u>retreated</u> into their homes.
b) The silversmith expertly fashioned a <u>delicate</u> flower pendant, each with exceptionally <u>fragile</u> petals.
c) (<u>dissent</u> altercation subordination)
   (discord <u>acceptance</u> refusal)
   (attraction <u>fascination</u> adoration)
   (<u>disinterest</u> disappointment boredom)
   (whisper <u>secrete</u> divulge)
   (sigh misplace <u>expose</u>)
Challenge 4
resolute is to determined as timid is to fainthearted
fragile is to robust as faint is to strong
seed is to sow as bulb is to plant
noun is to adjective as verb is to adverb
Now Try This!
1. resilient   vulnerable
2. flog   thrash
3. seek   catch

Pages 68–69
Challenge 1
crossover
deadline
threadbare
brainwash
comedown
counterpart
pinpoint
downbeat
Challenge 2
a) greed   (the other four can be verbs as well as nouns)
b) lovely   (the other four are adverbs)
c) chameleon   (the other four are mammals)
d) hilarious   (the other four are similar in meaning)
e) apparition   (the other four are similar in meaning)
f) ear   (the other four are joints)
Challenge 3
Answers may vary. Examples:
a) mindset   b) checkpoint
c) proofread   d) landslide
Challenge 4
a) tornado   hurricane
b) tomato   apple
c) transporter   freighter
d) comet   asteroid
e) drop   fall
f) escalate   raise
Now Try This!
1. a) foot   age
   b) black   list
2. a) hospital   clinic
   b) cuboid   cylinder
   c) see   observe

d) pleasant   fine
e) strike   attack

Pages 70–71
Challenge 1
a) l   earl, cull   b) k   sick, bank
c) p   clasp, grip   d) k   kink, rack
e) t   stunt, closet   f) y   tally, spiny
g) e   suite, mete   h) t   rant, tint
i) e   vane, ride   j) d   weird, beard
Challenge 2
a) w   whack, wrap   b) s   strip, scare
c) s   slate, stack   d) w   when, welder
e) s   spirit, stride   f) f   flunk, frail
g) g   grave, gravel   h) b   bawl, brawn
i) g   grope, grain   j) b   blame, beige
Challenge 3
a) p   grasp, pulse
b) b   bulb, brooch
c) t   silt, threat
d) k   flank, knack
Challenge 4
a) The word is **DEBT**
b) i) +6, −6   ii) −5, −2
Now Try This!
1. a) D   GN
   (+4, −4)
   b) E   HS
   (+1, −1)
2. a) t   b) h

Pages 72–73
Challenge 1
a) group   b) lithe
Challenge 2
a) A = 3, N = 2, E = 4, I = 5, L = 6
b) 63271524
Challenge 3
ARE YOU A CODE CRACKER?
Challenge 4
3rd JANUARY
SORRY I MISSED YOU! LOVING THE JEWELS. THE BLACK PANTHER XX
P.S. CATCH ME IF YOU CAN!
Now Try This!
1. FLAKE
   SNOW to TPRA is +1, +2, +3, +4, so reverse to −1, −2, −3, −4, −5 to find the word that GNDOJ is the code for.
2. FOANN
   Back 6 letters, forward 6 letters, back 6 letters, forward 6 letters, and so on.
3. a) 4256   b) PALE

Pages 74–75
Challenge 1
a) SATURATE   b) MYTHOLOGICAL
c) INFURIATE   d) PROCURE
Challenge 2
The seven-letter word is **weather**.
Challenge 3
a) +5, 10, 15, 20, 25 (increasing at each step in multiples of 5, starting from 5)
b) Square the number, halve the number
c) Halving every alternate number
d) Increasing by 2 every alternate number / increasing by 3 every alternate number
Challenge 4
a) 1st letter +4, 2nd letter −4
b) 1st letter −2, −4, −8, −16 (double the previous number), 2nd letter +3, +6, +12, +24 (double the previous number)

Now Try This!
1. a) 98
   +3, +6, +12, +24, so +48 = 98 (doubling the jump each time)
   b) 19
   First number to third is –6; second number to fourth is –4. So, 23 – 4 = 19
2. a) UA
   1st letter +4, 2nd letter –5
   b) WG
   +4 on alternating pairs

Pages 76–77
Challenge 1
a) 84 ÷ (2 × 3) + 6 = 20
b) (11 – 2) × 4 + 5 = 41
c) (150 × 2) – (25 ÷ 5) = 295
d) (58 + 12) ÷ 5 × 4 = 56
Challenge 2
Numbers that should have a square around them: 4, 9, 16, 25, 36, 49, 64, 81, 100, 121, 144, 225, 400
Numbers that should have a circle around them: 8, 27, 64, 125, 216, 343
Challenge 3
Possible answers are:
a) 7 × 8 + 4   (7 + 8) × 4
b) 6 × 5 + 3   (6 + 5) × 3
c) 32 – 16 + 4   32 ÷ 16 × 10
Challenge 4
a) C ÷ A × D + E – B = B
b) (B – E) × (B ÷ A) = E
Now Try This!
1. a) A
   (4 × 20) ÷ 5 – 12 = 4
   b) C
   20 ÷ 5 × 4 – 4 = 12
2. a) 5   b) 192
3. a) 6
   1st number divided by 2nd number, then halve the answer.
   b) 216
   Multiply the 1st and 3rd numbers, then cube the answer.

Pages 78–79
Challenge 1
a) 3 times
b) Sol
c) D   Neither i nor ii
Challenge 2

	Cat	Dog	Rabbit	Goldfish	Hamster	Gerbil	Lizard
Leo	x	x	xx				xx
Ellis				x	x	xx	
Sunita			xx	xx		x	
Dav	xx					x	

Leo has the most pets.
Challenge 3
A   William is Charlie's grandfather
     If William is Charlie's father's father, he must be Charlie's grandfather.

Challenge 4
a) Claire
   The fact that 'four of the chefs use carrots' is irrelevant as Claire would still use the fewest ingredients.

	Claire	Ralf	Parvis	Jake	Nell
Potatoes		x	x	x	
Carrots					
Chicken	x	x	x	x	
Fish					x
Flour	x	x		x	x
Salt		x	x	x	x
Onions			x		x
Mushrooms			x		

b) C   The brown dogs have blue eyes.
Now Try This!
C   Hanami arrived at 6:30 pm.

Hanami	Anna	Ben	Duncan	Keir
6:30	7:15	6:00	7:05	6:45

Pages 80–83
1. wet is to sodden as arid is to dry
   gallant is to chivalrous as imbecility is to absurdity
   lacklustre is to inspired as feeble is to strong
2. Any from: veg, get, table, let, able, tab, lab, gable, teal, bleat, veal, leave, vale, vat, bat, leg, lag, beg, bag, bet
   [1 mark for each four words]
3. **Answers will vary. Examples:**
   Mum's green eyes **complement** her new green coat.
   I paid Mum a **compliment** for baking such a great cake.
   Flooding tends to **affect** the same low-lying areas every year.
   The **effect** of the heavy flooding was devastating.
4. plentiful   abundant
5. mast tilt / mask kilt / mass silt
   flit tent / flip pent
   plop prop / plod drop
6. foot
7. A   Isaac is in the choir.
8. a) F
   (8 × 5) ÷ 4 – 7 = 3
   b) D
   2 × (4 ÷ 8) + 4 = 5
9. a) 11
   The left side of the equation equals 99.
   b) 9
   The left side of the equation equals 65.
10. dictatorship   democracy
11. a) DF
    Mirror pairs
    b) HL
    1st letter –4, 2nd letter –3
12. First, he takes the goat across. He returns alone and then takes the wolf across, but comes back with the goat. Then he takes the cabbage across, leaving it with the wolf and returns alone to get the goat.

13. a) 3156   b) 4521
    c) CASH   d) PACE
14. a) derive / drivel   b) pilot
    c) chief   d) frame / flame
    e) portion   f) crowns / crowds
15. BD
    1st letter –6, 2nd letter +8
16. IO
    1st letter +1, 0, –1, –2, –3, 2nd letter –1, –2, –3, –4, –5
17. cast
18. 2nd word is formed from the 8th, 5th and 3rd letter from the 1st word.
19. a) disagree   concur
    b) breathe   think
20. a) tint, tome, moth
    b) dome, tall, sand
    c) myth, joys, real (also: dare)
21. a) tentative   uncertain
    b) follow   trail

Non-Verbal Reasoning Activities

Pages 84–85
Challenge 1
Drawings should include all of the features listed.
a) The shapes have the following in common:
   • Rectangular shape
   • Divided into triangles the same shape
   • Patterns made up of four small shapes, which are repeated at either end of each rectangle
b) The shapes have the following in common:
   • Same overall area
   • Divided into six equal sections
   • Two black dots in one section, a cross in two sections, a circle in one section
Challenge 2
a) A, W, V, T, M have only vertical symmetry; B, E, K, C, D have only horizontal symmetry; H, I, O have both horizontal and vertical symmetry.
b) S is the odd one out as it has no symmetry.
Challenge 3
All of the figures are made up of the same shape with just the position of the two dots and the colours changing.
Now Try This!
1. C
   All the images on the left are made up of a square with one curved corner and curved lines running through the opposite corner to the curved corner of the square.
2. C
   The images on the left are all isosceles triangles divided by a line running parallel to the shortest side of the triangle, with a dot in the same place on the right-hand side of the triangle as it sits upright on the shortest side.
3. B
   The images on the left all show arrows going clockwise, with a black dot on the section before the arrowhead.

4. A

The images on the left are all made up of seven lines and have a vertical line of symmetry.

Pages 86–87

Challenge 1

a) The chickens have the following in common:
- Their bodies are made up of the same three triangles arranged identically.
- Legs are the same.
- All have the same number of scallops at the top as the number of sides in the polygon of its wing.
- The pattern in the parallel lines in the 'tail' triangle matches the pattern on the 'stomach' part of the chicken.

b) It is the only one with an irregular polygon for its wing.

Challenge 2

a) The trees have in common:
- All made up of a pot, stem and tree section.
- All have quadrilateral pots.
- All divided by parallel lines across the 'tree'.

b) Possible answers are:
A is the only option with the smallest inverted shape at the top.
B is the only option with the stem divided by three horizontal lines.
C is the only one with three pairs of parallel lines in the tree section.
D is the only one with no line between the 'tree' and the 'stem'.

Challenge 3

a) Each flowerbed is made up of six units (i.e. has the same area). Each flower has one more petal than the total number of flowers there are. Each flowerbed has red roses.

b) Odd ones out would be B and D (top middle and bottom left-hand side) as they are the only two beds without symmetry.

c) New beds drawn should meet the criteria above.

Now Try This!

1. **A**
The only option with striped shading in the triangle running diagonal to the sides rather than perpendicular/parallel.

2. **C**
The only option with two diagonal lines on faces.

3. **E**
The only option with the circles touching different sides of the semicircle and cutting across the semicircle, rather than both touching the same side of the semicircle around the edge as in all the other figures.

Pages 88–89

Challenge 1

Answers as follows from the top of page 88:
DO
(C = triangles arranged so that they touch

at a point; D = triangles arranged so they touch by a side; P = dots touching like a flower; Q = dots vertical; O = dots diagonal)
GS
(E = black rectangle; F = rectangle black at either end and open in the middle; H = open rectangle; G = rectangle open at either end and black in the middle; R = green rectangle equally divided into four; S = green rectangle divided into 2 upper sections and 3 lower ones; T = green rectangle divided into 3 upper sections and 2 lower ones)
LO
(M = three shapes inside one another; N = no shapes inside one another; L = two shapes inside one another; O = open moon facing left; P = black moon facing right; Q = black moon facing left)
VE
(W = starting with the top shape and moving clockwise, the shapes are square, circle, flower and triangle; V = starting with the top shape and moving clockwise, the shapes are triangle, flower, circle and square; E = top triangle shaded; F = bottom triangle shaded; G = both triangles shaded)
WA
(W = diamond shape; V = pentagon facing upwards; X = pentagon facing downwards; A = vertical shading; B = crosshatch shading; C = horizontal shading)
LK
(Q = number; L = letter; I = no symmetry; J = vertical symmetry; K = horizontal symmetry)
SA
(S = triangle in the top left corner is shaded towards the corner of the figure;
Y = triangle in the top left corner is shaded towards the middle of the figure;
B = bottom line is vertical; A = bottom line is diagonal)
ND
(Z = top right circle has a fine line; U = top right circle is dashed; N = top right circle is bold; I = top right circle is dotted
E = all three semicircles have a bold line crossing them; D = left-hand semicircles have a bold line crossing them; F = right-hand semicircles have a bold line crossing them)
CA
(D = horizontal bold line on left side of figure; C = no bold line on left side of the figure; Q = sideways, bold v-shape on left side of the figure; A = heart in the orange shaded section; B = heart in blue shaded section; O = heart outside shaded sections)
TS
(U = fine diagonal line goes from top left to bottom middle; T = fine diagonal line goes from bottom left to top middle; R = horizontal line is below the bold lines; S = horizontal line is above the bold line)
LO
(R = three pairs of branches; L = four pairs of branches; S = five pairs of branches; P = trapezium pot; X = square pot; O = rectangular pot)
VE
(X = bold outline; V = 'bubble writing' outline; Y = dashed outline; A = no

symmetry; Z = horizontal symmetry only; E = vertical and horizontal symmetry)
FI
(F = two shapes inside one another; G = all three shapes inside one another; H = no shapes inside each other; I = bold vertical line; J = fine vertical line)
SH
(S = dot below the curved line; G = no dot; C = dot inside the curved line; N = diagonal cross inside pink box; H = vertical/horizontal cross inside pink box; C = horizontal stripes inside pink box)
The code should read DOGS LOVE WALKS AND CATS LOVE FISH.

Pages 90–91

Challenge 1

Answers as follows from the top of page 90:
HIS
(F = large arrow shape points to top left; G = large arrow shape points to top right; H = large arrow shape points to bottom right; I = square on left side of figure; J = square on right side of figure;
R = circle at top of figure; S = circle at bottom of figure)
REV
(S = arrow pointing left; R = arrow pointing right; E = large open arrowhead; F = large black arrowhead;
G = fine arrowhead; W = figure's lowest point is in the middle; V = figure's lowest point is on the right side)
GEO
(G = star in the blue section of the semicircle; H = circle in the blue section of the semicircle; D = open circle; E = black circle; O = semicircle has the flat side at the base; P = semicircle has the curved side at the base)
TKI
(T = star has a diagonal line through it; S = star has a horizontal line through it; R = star has a vertical line through it; N = triangle has a dash in it; K = triangle does not have a dash in it; I = circle has a dot in it; J = rectangle has a dot in it)
MBN
(M = arrow pointing into the shape; W = arrow pointing out of the shape; A = arrow pointing left; B = arrow pointing right; P = horizontal line; N = vertical line)
EHN
(G = upper dot on right side of figure; F = upper dot at top of figure; E = upper dot on left of figure; H = circle at bottom of figure divided into two; I = circle at bottom of figure divided into three; M = lower dot on right side of figure; N = lower dot on left side of figure)
The note should read THIS IS REVENGE FOR TAKING MY BONE. HENRY.

Challenge 2

Answers as follows from the top of page 91:
UND
(V = outer shape has five sides; U = outer shape has six sides; N = shape divided into two; M = shape divided into three; O = shape divided into four; E = dashed line at top of figure; D = dashed line at bottom of figure)

ERC
(E = rectangle is horizontal; F = rectangle is vertical; P = line with a dot is on the left side; R = line with a dot is on the right side; A = oval inside the orange shape; B = oval is inside the small rectangle inside the orange shape; C = oval outside the orange shape)
HER
(G = large shape is a triangle; H = large shape is a hexagon; D = solid circle
E = dashed circle; V = square inside circle; R = square outside circle)
RYB
(T = three loops in arrow; R = four loops in arrow; Y = single line at end of arrow; N = double line at end of arrow; B = large open arrowhead; A = large black arrowhead; C = fine arrowhead)
USH
(U = open arrowhead; X = black arrowhead; S = bold line furthest from the arrowhead; Q = bold line closest to arrowhead; H = fine line closest to arrowhead; T = fine line furthest from arrowhead)
The completed answers should read UNDER CHERRY BUSH.

Pages 92–93
Challenge 1
a) i) They have been reflected.
   ii) Dot added on top and pole no longer visible in rectangle of the boat.
   iii) White triangles have disappeared.
b) i) Large red sail has moved across to the right-hand side of the boat.
   ii) The pink section is divided into two not three; the stripes have changed from horizontal to vertical.
c) i) Dot added on top.
   ii) Division has swapped from diagonal to horizontal; scallops have changed to zigzags.
   iii) Bold line has disappeared; small blue triangles at the top have been added; triangles at the sides have been merged with the boat; horizontal dividing line has appeared.
Challenge 2
a) Answer should include: fish becomes smaller; two concentric triangles in the tail; seven scallops in the tail; three gill lines each side.
b) Answer should include: fish rotated 90 degrees anticlockwise; six perpendicular lines on tail; four squares with circles inside them; crossed lines on fish's body.
Challenge 3
a) D
   Each fish gains two bubbles and the seaweed appears.
b) B
   The coral gains two extra branches and one extra dot.
Now Try This!
1. E
   Each image moves one place anticlockwise around the edge.
2. D
   The second image is the mirror image of the first each time.

Pages 94–95
Challenge 1
a) The missing tile should look like the bottom right-hand tile, reflected in a vertical mirror line.
b) The missing tile should have the blue square in it, with a dot in the top right-hand corner.
Challenge 2
a) The missing tile should be a mirror image of the one in the bottom right of the grid
b) The missing tile should have a rectangle in the top left-hand corner and an L-shape in the bottom right-hand corner. The bold line should move to the left-hand side. The wavy line should move upwards in the grid. There should be a double > shape in the centre.
Challenge 3
Various answers possible.
Now Try This!
1. A
   Moving from left to right, the figures change as the shading rotates 90 degrees. The irregular polygons increase by one side in each row of the grid moving from left to right.
2. B
   The missing tile should have a hexagon reflected in a horizontal mirror line (so it would not change from the bottom left of the grid), the arrow having swapped direction and the dashed line having moved inside the polygon at the top.
3. A
   The missing tile should have a star with seven points (the points increase by one in each row moving left to right), two lines in the top right-hand corner (in each row there is a square with one line, two lines and three lines) and a tall rectangle in the bottom left-hand corner (these are consistent moving down each column).

Pages 96–97
Challenge 1
Answers should reflect the following rules:
a) The scalloped and fine line should continue on the diagonal. There should be three short lines across the left-hand outer edge of the hexagon. There should be three black circles and three open circles.
b) Moving anticlockwise around the outer hexagons, each figure moves one place anticlockwise.
c) Moving clockwise around the outer hexagons, starting with the top right-hand side, the number of triangles increases by one. Moving clockwise around the outer hexagons, starting with the left-hand side, the number of circles increases by one. Moving anti-clockwise around the outer hexagons, starting with the top right-hand side, the number of crosses increases by 1 up to 3 and then back to 1.
d) Each bold black line continues throughout the grid.
e) The number of circles increases by 1 each time moving clockwise around

the hexagon from the left-hand side hexagon with a single dot. The number of lines nearest the central hexagon increases by 1 each time moving clockwise around the hexagon from the bottom left-hand hexagon with a single line nearest the central hexagon. The outer line nearest the outside of the figure in each small hexagon cycles between bold, dashed and dotted, repeating around the edge of the figure.
f) Each set of shapes should match the configuration of those in the opposite hexagon.
Challenge 2
Various answers possible.
Challenge 3
Answers should reflect the following rules:
a) The centre lines match those of the opposite octagon. The position of the asterisk is the same relative to its position in the opposite octagon. The triangles move clockwise from octagon to octagon.
b) Moving anticlockwise around the octagons from the top centre, the scallop moves two corners anticlockwise. The dot moves one corner clockwise.
Now Try This!
1. C
   Each centre column figure is composed of the two either side overlapping, with no shading.
2. B
   Moving from left to right along the top row, then dropping down to move right to left along the middle row, then dropping down and moving left to right along the bottom row, the semicircle rotates 90 degrees clockwise. The square moves between right-middle-left-middle-right of the semicircle. Imagining each semicircle sitting upright, the short line in the square alternates between pointing to the right and left of the semicircle.
3. A
   Moving from left to right at the bottom of the grid, the dot moves diagonally to the other corner of the square. The number of arches increases to six on the right-hand side of the grid and rotates one corner anticlockwise.

Pages 98–99
Challenge 1
a) Top and bottom rows flow together: moving from left to right, black square moves one section clockwise each time; clover alternates between top right-hand square (top row) and right-hand triangle (bottom row).
b) Top and bottom rows flow together: moving from left to right, V-shape moves from left to right. Top row: bold short line is horizontal. Arrows mirror each other in each figure. Arrowheads consistent (all bold). Bottom row: bold short line is vertical. Arrows mirror each other in each figure. Arrowheads consistent (all open).

Challenge 2
a) All the figures in blue are the same, so answer should be identical to other blue figures.
b) The answer should have a bold line at the bottom, dashes that fit the sequence (they are reducing in size with each pink triangle) and four scallops.
c) The answer should have horizontal shading to the right-hand side of the vertical line, three squares on the left-hand side of the vertical line and a small square with a line to the top left-hand side.

Challenge 3
Answers will vary.

Now Try This!
1. B
Moving from left to right, the V-shape moves gradually clockwise around the circle and one additional scallop is added.
2. E
Moving from left to right, each line becomes gradually thicker and the pattern continues as new fine lines are added.
3. C
Moving from left to right, the number of black dots increases by 1. The curved line moves from left to right in each square. The bold lines at the bottom of each square alternate between a cross, an L-shape and a T-shape.
4. B
Moving from left to right, the bold lines alternate between low and high; the dots alternate between 1 and 2; the crosses turn one at a time to a circle and then disappear.

Pages 100–101
Challenge 1
The answer should show the figures appearing as the paper is unfolded. First the figures will be mirrored as the paper is folded down along its horizontal edge; then the hexagon should be shown appearing on the bottom left-hand corner; then the hexagon should appear in the top left-hand corner.

Challenge 2
a) The unfolded paper should have a heart in the top right-hand corner (but not the bottom right-hand corner) and two circles central on the left-hand side.
b) The unfolded paper should have two hearts arranged on the left-hand side arranged vertically (the bottom one upside down), two hearts horizontally in the middle of the top side with the points facing outward, two squares either side of the central diagonal line and two hearts in the bottom right-hand corner arranged with their points inwards.

Challenge 3
Answers will vary.

Challenge 4
a) Clover and spiral; leaf and star; circle and heart.
b) Dots and semiquaver; star and quaver; treble clef and bass clef.

c) Sun and diamond; moon and circle; daisy and three dots.
d) Diamond and moon; dots and circle; semiquaver and quaver.
e) Bass clef and triangle; treble clef and daisy; spiral and diamond.
f) Star and circles; moon and dots; circle and sun.
g) Clover and daisy; spiral and diamond; circle and bass clef.
h) Five-point star and sun; heart and leaf; circle and four-point star.
i) Circle and heart; star and leaf; clover and moon.
j) Daisy and treble clef; moon and dots; semiquaver and heart.
k) Clover and four-point star; heart and sun; moon and dots.

Now Try This!
1. C
2. E

Pages 102–103
Challenge 1
i = D   ii = A   iii = F
Challenge 2
i = B   ii = A   iii = D
Challenge 3
The blocks should show (all arranged horizontally): two squares; five squares; three squares; three squares
Now Try This!
1. B
2. E

Pages 104–108
1. a) B
Moving from left to right, the cross is added to the large shape and the lines change to dots. The large shape is reflected in a vertical mirror line.
   b) D
Moving from left to right, the short diagonal line is reflected vertically; the central triangle changes to a pentagon; the elongated triangle changes to an elongated oval.
2. a) E
Moving from left to right, the level of the horizontal line raises and lowers; the number of short vertical lines increases by one; the black dot moves one corner anticlockwise; the dashed line does not change.
   b) A
Moving from left to right across the sequence, one extra black dot is added. The dots remain in place once they are added and do not move.
3. a) E
Y = arrow points to side of rectangle; O = rectangle is diagonal
   b) E
V = seven petals; C = five petals coloured

4. a) E
Moving from left to right, the polygons become regular and the shading swaps to the inside polygon. The line outside the large polygon at the top moves inside the large polygon to the bottom. The line outside the large polygon at the bottom moves inside the large polygon at the top.
   b) E
Moving from left to right, the shading does not change. The image in the bottom right of the grid moves to the top left; the image in the top right of the grid rotates 90 degrees clockwise; the image in the bottom left of the grid moves to the bottom right and is reflected in a vertical mirror line; the image in the top left of the grid is reflected in a horizontal line and moves to the bottom left of the grid.
5. a) D
In each image on the left of the question, the small shapes follow the same order moving clockwise around the edge.
   b) E
Both images on the left-hand side are identical but rotated.
6. a) D
All the other images have three dividing lines.
   b) D
In all the other figures, the black circle is between the white circle and the perpendicular line.
7. a) A   b) C
8. i) C   ii) A   iii) B
9. a) A   b) C   c) E

Pages 109–124: Mathematics Test Paper
1 E
$2{,}403 \times 3 = 7{,}209$
2 B
Decimal point moving one to the right (62.45 to 624.5) and then two to the left (193.2 to 1.932), so move the decimal point one to the left to go from 12,065.34 to 1,206.534
3 C
Ranjeet owns $6 + 6 + 3$,
Colin $6 + 6 + 6 + 3$ and Pete $6 + 6 + 6$.
Total toys = $15 + 21 + 18 = 54$.
To get the mean: $54 \div 3$ people = 18 toys
4 D
Add the two numbers previous, so $15 + 34 = 49$
5 D
12 shaded out of 20, so to get the percentage multiply the top and bottom of the fraction by 5 to get $\frac{60}{100}$ so 60%.
6 A
15% of 200p = $0.15 \times 200 = 30$p. A quarter of £6 = $6 \div 4 = 1.5$, so £1.50 + 30p = £1.80
7 B
Decimal point has moved three to the left so must be multiplying by 0.001

8 C

So journey = 18 minutes + 37 minutes + 13 minutes = 68 minutes.
68 minutes before 8:34 am = 7:26 am

9 E

Remember the hour hand will be halfway between 2 and 3. There are 30 degrees every 5 minutes (as 360 ÷ 12 = 30) so 30 + 30 + 30 + 15 = 105

10 C

A regular octagon has interior angles of 135 degrees. 8 sides minus 2 = 6.
6 × 180 = 1080. 1080 ÷ 8 sides = 135

11 B

So 6 × 1 × 1 = 6 cubic metres = 6,000 litres

12 A

83 and 89 are the prime numbers.

13 B

(4, 4) reflected in the y-axis moves to (–4, 4).

14 D

So £8.50 × 14 = £119, £564 × 0.05 = £28.20, £119 + £28.20 = £147.20

15 C

68.32 – 19.39 = 48.93

16 A

180 degrees on a straight line. Ratio 3 : 1, add ratios to get 4.
180 ÷ 4 = 45, 45 × 3 = 135

17 C

90 degrees clockwise from North East is South East.

18 D

Unify units to get 120,000 ÷ 400 = 300

19 D

Shortest journey time from London to Newcastle is Train 2. 1049 to 1503 = 4 hours and 14 minutes. Delay of 37 minutes so 4 hours and 51 minutes.

20 E

A triangular prism has 5 faces, 9 edges and 6 vertices.

21 C

Given sides = 9 + 18 + 24 + 10 = 61, missing sides = (18 – 10) + (24 – 9) = 23, 23 + 61 = 84 m

22 D

(10 × 24) + (9 × 8) = 240 + 72 = 312

23 A

Two-fifths of the run was 3 miles. So 3 ÷ 2 = 1.5 miles = one-fifth.
So 5 × 1.5 = 7.5 miles

24 B

(3 × 80p) + (2 × 1.45) + £1.90 = £2.40 + £2.90 + £1.90 = £7.20.
£10 – £7.20 = £2.80

25 D

They weren't moving between 9:00 and 10:00 so 1 hour.

26 A

7:00 to 13:00 = 6 hours. They travelled 6 miles in total so an average speed of 1 mph.

27 B

$\frac{3}{7}$ left after the friends ate their share.
$\frac{3}{5} \times \frac{3}{7} = \frac{9}{35}$ eaten by me. So $\frac{9}{35} + \frac{4}{7} = \frac{29}{35}$ eaten and $\frac{6}{35}$ left.

28 D

Unify the units so 0.7 × 0.3 × 0.5 = 0.105 m³

29 C

7 + 7 + 7 + 7 = 28 m

30 B

$\frac{72}{x} = \frac{60}{100}$. Multiply both sides by 100 to get $\frac{7,200}{x} = 60$. $\frac{7,200}{60} = x$, x = 120

31 B

2.0012 is closest to 2

32 E

It's 8 × 8 × 8 × 8 so 4,096

33 C

Do the reverse, so 125 × 2 = 250, 250 – 75 = 175, 175 ÷ 5 = 35

34 D

Let cola = C and pencils = P. 4C + 5P = £3.65 and 2C + 6P = £2.70. Double the latter equation to get 4C + 12P = £5.40. Subtract the first equation to get 7P = £1.75, P = 25p

35 A

The ratio is 8 : 4 : 1. Add the ratios to get 13.195 ÷ 13 = 15, 15 × 4 = 60

36 D

(34 × 20p) + (7 × £1) = £13.80, £23.30 – £13.80 = £9.50, £9.50 ÷ 50p = 19

37 B

Unify the units so 350 × 400 = 140,000. 140,000 ÷ (70 × 20) = 100

38 E

(6 × 30.5) + (3 × 2.5) = 183 + 7.5 = 190.5 cm or 1.905 m.

39 D

£1,350 × 0.8 = £1,080
£1,080 – £720 = £360

40 B

It's a kite.

41 C

April has 30 days, so 30 days between the two dates. 4 × 7 = 28 so add two days and get Friday.

42 C

Grandmother must be 68 + 23 = 91. I am 91 – 74 = 17, so 12 years ago = 5

43 D

Bus percentage = 100 – 29 – 23 – 32 = 16. 16% is half of 32% for Car so 226 ÷ 2 = 113

44 A

Subtracting by one more each time, so 24 – 36 = –12

45 C

BIDMAS, so 13 + (45) – 7 + (48) = 99

46 B

So 11:47 pm in Bahrain = 9:47 pm in the UK. 9:47 pm minus 6 hours and 24 minutes = 3:23 pm

47 D

5x + 2y + 5x + 2y + 3x + y + 3x + y = 16x + 6y

48 A

(5x + 2y)(3x + y)
= 5x(3x + y) + 2y(3x + y)
= 15x² + 11xy + 2y²

49 B

Surface area of cube = 3 × 3 = 9, 9 × 6 = 54, so 54 ÷ 3 = 18, 18 × 15 = 270, so 4 and a half hours.

50 A

7 is the highest single figure prime number and 9 is the highest single figure square number, so 797.

Pages 125–136: English Test Paper Comprehension

1. E   An embankment for the train to run through higher ground
The cutting is where the high ground has been cut through for the train to run level.

2. B   The signalman looks in a different direction to the speaker
We are told the signalman looks down the railway line rather than upwards to where the speaker is on the higher ground.

3. B   He was silhouetted and, due to perspective, seemed shorter
We are told he is 'foreshortened and shadowed' by the light and position of the two men.

4. D   He makes a gesture
He gestures with the flag to show the way down the steep slope.

5. C   Steep and slippery
The cutting is 'steep' and the path is 'unusually precipitate'.

6. A   His face is unhealthy-looking and he is highly alert
The signalman is 'sallow' and is described as waiting with 'watchfulness'

7. E   You could not see as far into the distance toward the tunnel's mouth
We are told there is a 'shorter perspective' in that direction.

8. B   He presumes the job is isolating; therefore, he is hopeful of being welcome
'A visitor was a rarity, I should suppose; not an unwelcome rarity, I hoped?'

9. A   Fascinated, as he has previously had a very sheltered existence
'In me, he merely saw a man who had been shut up within narrow limits all his life, and who, being at last set free, had a newly-awakened interest in these great works.'

10. A   We see he is highly nervous and may be mentally ill
The signalman is jumpy and on edge, and the narrator wonders if there is an 'infection' in his mind.

11. C   Mentally taxing but physically light
The job has almost no 'manual labour' but requires the signalman to be alert.

12. B   He has become accustomed to the isolation
'Regarding those many long and lonely hours of which I seemed to make so much, he could only say that the routine of his life had shaped itself into that form, and he had grown used to it.'

13. A   Unnerving and ominous
The signalman is so on edge at the narrator's arrival, and is so scared that he may have seen him before, it creates an ominous atmosphere.

14. E   Sensory description
The writer describes what can be seen, smelt and felt.

15. C   He has an interest in the railways
He has an interest in 'these great works'.

16. **C** Relieved
    They both feel their 'manner cleared'.
17. **A** First person
    The narrator writes as 'I' but does not know more than his companion.
18. **B** Steep
19. **D** The processes involved with the railways; industrialisation
20. **B** He is terrified of what might be about to happen
    The signalman can barely speak because he is scared that the narrator is an apparition.
21. **A** Sombre
22. **C** Dormant
23. **D** Nouns
24. **B** Adjectives
25. **A** Noun

Spelling
26. **C** escalator
    An 'x' has been added after 'e'.
27. **A** eruption
    There is only one 'r'.
28. **D** admission
    There is only one 'd'.
29. **B** allowed
    The homophone 'aloud' has been used.
30. **D** deal
    The vowel digraph 'ee' has been used instead of 'ea'.
31. **A** sombre
    This word is 'borrowed' from the French, meaning 'dark'.
32. **C** software
    The homophone 'wear' has been used.
33. **N** There is no mistake.

Punctuation
34. **C** Its
    An apostrophe has been added to make *It's* ('It is').
35. **C** The drip,
    A semi-colon has been inserted instead of a comma.
36. **C** water's
    An apostrophe is required to make *water's* ('water is').
37. **A** We'll
    An apostrophe is required to make *We'll* ('We will').
38. **N** There is no mistake.
39. **A** cave's
    An apostrophe is required to indicate possession.
40. **B** then
    A semi-colon is not followed by a capital letter.
41. **C** night,"
    The final inverted commas should come after the final punctuation in the direct speech.

Grammar
42. **C** was taken
    The passive form of the verb phrase 'to take unawares'.
43. **A** whom
    The object form of the relative pronoun 'who'.
44. **E** but
    The phrase is 'anything but'.

45. **E** her
    The possessive determiner 'her', modifying 'money'.
46. **B** to
    The preposition 'to' is the only one that makes sense.
47. **C** a
    The indefinite article 'a' is the only one that makes sense before the noun 'bit' in this context.
48. **A** whispered
    Only the simple past tense makes sense in this context.
49. **B** should
    No other modal verb makes sense in this context.

Pages 137–152: Verbal Reasoning Test Paper
1. **C** IQUR
   Each letter +1, +2, +3, +4
2. **E** HGZWRFN
   Mirror code for PLAYER is KOZBVI; mirror code for STADIUM is HGZWRFN
3. **D** QUEUE
   Each letter −5, −4, −3, −2, −1, so find word by adding 5, 4, 3, 2, 1
4. **B** URANUS
   Each letter 0, −3, −6, −9, −12, −15, so find word by adding 0, 3, 6, 9, 12, 15
5. **A** DGJBLDO
   +1, −1
6. **B** NINETY
   −3, +3
7. **C** 8
   Terms in the 2nd, 4th, 6th, 8th positions decrease by 16, 14, 12, 10, …
8. **C** 120
   ×1, ×2, ×3, ×4, ×5
9. **E** 21
   Two sequences: alternate numbers −6, −5, −4, −3; then +3, +4, +5
10. **B** 64
    Ascending in prime numbers: +2, +3, +5, +7, +11, +13, then +17
11. **B** 37
    Adding the two previous numbers together
12. **D** 169
    Squares of prime numbers: $13^2 = 169$
13. **D** 2159
14. **E** LOST
15. **A** 32598
16. **D** 1526
17. **C** EAST
18. **B** 364512
19. **C** her **aft**er   raft
20. **B** Ger**man** yet   many
21. **D** edit**ed it**   edit
22. **C** inter**val e**veryone   vale
23. **C** **bus k**nows   busk
24. **B** ca**ble d**angled   bled
25. **A** reviled
    Words spelt backwards
26. **A** dub
    5th letter, 3rd letter, 1st letter
27. **B** rage
    Remove 1st and 4th letters
28. **C** broom
    1st letter, 7th letter, 3rd letter, 4th letter, 5th letter
29. **D** lyre
    6th and 7th letters followed by 5th and 4th

30. **B** rune
    Last letter, 2nd letter, 4th letter and 5th letter
31. **E** Willow finished last.
    As Ronan came second, then Andrew must have been first because he finished before him. Ted wasn't last so he was either third or fourth. As Sorcha finished before Ted (who wasn't last), she must have finished third.
32. **A** c
33. **D** t
34. **C** k
35. **E** y
36. **A** n
37. **E** p
38. **B** B
39. **E** E
40. **E** E
41. **B** B
42. **D** D
43. **E** E
44. **E** IR
    +4, −4
45. **B** CI
    +5, +5
46. **A** CB
    Mirror pairs
47. **D** HS
    +6 , −6
48. **A** CY
    +12, −6
49. **E** WT
    Mirror pairs
50. **C and X**
51. **B and Y**
52. **A and X**
53. **C and Y**
54. **A and Y**
55. **B and Z**
56. **A and Z**
57. **B and Z**
58. **A and Z**
59. **A and Y**
60. **B and Z**
61. **C and Y**
62. **C and Y**
63. **A and Y**
64. **B and X**
65. **B and Z**
66. **B and X**
67. **C and Z**
68. **A** EL
    1st letter +3, then −4 alternately; 2nd letter −2, −1, 0, +1, +2
69. **C** UQ
    1st letter +3, −2 alternately; 2nd letter +2, −3 alternately.
70. **B** NG
    1st letter −1, −2, −3, −4, −5; 2nd letter +2, −1, +2, −1, +2
71. **E** IJ
    1st letter +5, +4, +3, +2, +1; 2nd letter −4, −3, −2, −1, 0
72. **D** NW
    1st letter +1, −3 alternately; 2nd letter −1, 0, +1, +2, +3
73. **B** EL
    1st letter +3, then −4 alternately; 2nd letter −2, −1, 0, +1, +2
74. **A** 27
    1st number divided by 2, then add 3rd number.

75. **C** 9

Multiply the outside numbers to get square numbers, then find square root.

76. **D** 19

To find middle number, double the 1st and subtract from 3rd.

77. **E** 25

1st number multiplied by 3rd number divided by 9.

78. **A** 21

1st number divided by 3rd number +13.

79. **B** 324

1st number multiplied by 3rd number multiplied by 3.

80. **D** Sonny

Sonny only touches the tarantula and the bearded lizard.

Pages 153–168: Non-Verbal Reasoning Test Paper

Section 1

1 D
2 E
3 A
4 B
5 C
6 D
7 E
8 A
9 D
10 B
11 B
12 B

Section 2

1 **C**

In all the other figures, the number of perpendicular lines crossing the triangle is double the number of black squares in the triangle.

2 **B**

In all the other figures, the dashed diagonal line is on the end of the rectangle.

3 **B**

In all the other figures, the arrow goes through the smooth curved side of the large shape.

4 **C**

In all the other figures, the circle would be on the bottom left hand side of the semi-circle once the figure was rotated with the semi-circle's flat side 'sitting' horizontally at the base of the figure.

5 **C**

In all the other figures, the shading in the small shapes would be a line, then a circle, then blank (moving clockwise around the small figures starting with the small figure with a diagonal line).

6 **E**

In all the other figures, the inner shape is regular.

7 **D**

All the other figures have only one black circle per row.

8 **D**

In all the other figures, the square is higher than the rectangle.

9 **A**

In all the other figures, the small black triangle is the same shape and orientation as the area in which the dashed figure and the solid figure overlap.

10 **D**

In all the other figures, the figures follow the same order (starting with the heart, then square, star, circle, triangle, upside down heart, rectangle, flower) moving clockwise around the figure.

11 **E**

In all the other figures, the black side is below the vertical stripes.

12 **C**

In all the other figures, the plus and minus signs are aligned vertically.

Section 3

The hidden figure can be rotated but not reflected, and must be the same size as the shape shown on the left-hand side of the question.

1 D
2 E
3 B
4 C
5 B
6 A
7 D
8 A
9 C
10 A
11 D
12 B

Section 4

1 **C**

The figures on the left are composed of a stepped line with two identical small shapes (one each side of the line). The figure on the left of the stepped line is above the figure on the right-hand side of the stepped line.

2 **A**

The figures on the left are composed of an irregular hexagon with two bold sides, a dashed quadrilateral and a black shape which is positioned behind the other shapes in the figure.

3 **C**

The figures on the left both have an arrow positioned at the bottom right-hand side of a small rectangle, with a diagonal line also appearing in the figure.

4 **D**

The figures on the left both have an even number of sides in total.

5 **D**

The figures on the left both have a number of short perpendicular lines cutting through the outer shape equal to the number of circles inside the shape.

6 **E**

The figures on the left both have a larger shape and a medium-sized shape; the medium shape has three fewer sides than the large shape.

7 **A**

The figures on the left both have a small circle and a small cross directly opposite one another.

8 **A**

The figures on the left both have a white circle in the bottom right-hand

brick, a patterned shading in the bottom left-hand brick and a small black shape at the edge of one brick.

9 **D**

The figures on the left both have a grey shaded shape, overlapped by a white shape which is in its bottom right-hand corner. The white shape has one more side than the grey shape.

10 **A**

The figures on the left both comprise a shape crossed by a dashed line creating a quadrilateral and a dotted line creating a triangle. The dotted line is on the left hand side of the dashed line.

11 **B**

The figures on the left are both made up of four lines which cross in five places.

12 **A**

The figures on the left both have a line of symmetry running along the longest dimension of the figure; they have a black dot on the bottom right-hand side of the long figure if rotated to be vertical with the parallel perpendicular lines at the bottom.

Section 5

1 **A** OBX

E = flat ends on each bracket
O = arrows on each bracket
Q = twirled ends on each bracket
L = short bracket
B = long bracket
X = circle is inside the bracket
P = circle is outside the bracket

2 **B** DJO

D = triangles are different shading from one another
A = triangles are same shading as one another
G = upper triangle is white
H = upper triangle has diagonal striped shading
J = upper triangle has horizontal shading
I = L-shape has black ends
O = L-shape has white ends

3 **E** IRM

I = odd number of crosses
G = even number of crosses
K = black dot inside star is on right-hand side of figure
R = black dot inside star is on left-hand side of figure
M = black dot outside star at top right-hand side
N = black dot outside star at middle right-hand side
O = black dot outside star at bottom

4 **A** FKW

F = zigzag scallops
U = curved scallops
J = six scallops
Q = eight scallops
K = seven scallops
W = dot in right-hand circle
Z = vertical line in right-hand circle
X = horizontal line in right-hand circle

5   B   MRT

L = brickwork pattern has two bricks on top and bottom row, three in the middle
M = brickwork pattern has three bricks on top and bottom row, two in the middle
N = brickwork pattern has two bricks on bottom rows, three on the top
P = black dot in top right-hand corner
Q = black dot in top left-hand corner
R = dot in middle of top row
S = dot is not below black triangle
T = dot is directly below black triangle

6   C   TU

T = white square
Y = white rectangle
U = dotted pentagon
Q = white pentagon
O = diagonally striped pentagon

7   E   LXD

L = black shape is on uppermost 'step'
A = black shape is on middle 'step'
C = black shape is on bottom 'step'
M = black shape is a circle
X = black shape is a triangle
D = 'flag' points inwards towards the 'steps'
E = 'flag' points outwards away from the 'steps'

8   D   CIS

E = large square divided from top left to bottom right
C = large square divided from top right to bottom left
I = white outlined section in large square falls in the top half
N = white outlined section in large square falls in the bottom half
R = small white square in top left-hand corner
S = small white square in top right-hand corner

9   A   VB

H = longest side of ice cream cone shape is vertical
V = longest side of ice cream cone shape is horizontal
B = black dot is in the 'ice cream' section
T = black dot is in the 'cone' section
A = black dot is outside the ice cream cone shape

10   A   HKL

F = black centre
G = white centre
H = dot in the centre
J = eight petals
K = five petals
L = oval at the top of the flower
M = pentagon at the top of the flower

11   A   FA

F = two scallops
X = three scallops
E = four scallops
U = three black circles
O = two black circles and one white circle
A = two black circles and two white circles

12   A   EN

B = diagonal striped shading running from bottom left to top right in the larger polygon
E = vertical striped shading in the larger polygon
Y = diagonal striped shading running from bottom right to top left in the larger polygon
S = arrow pointing towards the centre shape
M = arrow pointing away from the centre shape
N = double-headed arrow
O = no arrowheads

MATHEMATICS TEST PAPER

Pupil's Name

School Name

Date of Test

PUPIL NUMBER

[0]	[0]	[0]	[0]	[0]	[0]
[1]	[1]	[1]	[1]	[1]	[1]
[2]	[2]	[2]	[2]	[2]	[2]
[3]	[3]	[3]	[3]	[3]	[3]
[4]	[4]	[4]	[4]	[4]	[4]
[5]	[5]	[5]	[5]	[5]	[5]
[6]	[6]	[6]	[6]	[6]	[6]
[7]	[7]	[7]	[7]	[7]	[7]
[8]	[8]	[8]	[8]	[8]	[8]
[9]	[9]	[9]	[9]	[9]	[9]

SCHOOL NUMBER

[0]	[0]	[0]	[0]	[0]	[0]	[0]
[1]	[1]	[1]	[1]	[1]	[1]	[1]
[2]	[2]	[2]	[2]	[2]	[2]	[2]
[3]	[3]	[3]	[3]	[3]	[3]	[3]
[4]	[4]	[4]	[4]	[4]	[4]	[4]
[5]	[5]	[5]	[5]	[5]	[5]	[5]
[6]	[6]	[6]	[6]	[6]	[6]	[6]
[7]	[7]	[7]	[7]	[7]	[7]	[7]
[8]	[8]	[8]	[8]	[8]	[8]	[8]
[9]	[9]	[9]	[9]	[9]	[9]	[9]

Please mark like this ⊢.

DATE OF BIRTH

Day		Month	Year
[0]	[0]	January	2007
[1]	[1]	February	2008
[2]	[2]	March	2009
[3]	[3]	April	2010
	[4]	May	2011
	[5]	June	2012
	[6]	July	2013
	[7]	August	2014
	[8]	September	2015
	[9]	October	2016
		November	2017
		December	2018

1 A B C D E

2 A B C D E

3 A B C D E

4 A B C D E

5 A B C D E

6 A B C D E

7 A B C D E

8 A B C D E

9 A B C D E

10 A B C D E

11 A B C D E

12 A B C D E

13 A B C D E

14 A B C D E

15 A B C D E

16 A B C D E

17 A B C D E

18 A B C D E

19 A B C D E

20 A B C D E

21 A B C D E

22 A B C D E

23 A B C D E

24 A B C D E

25 A B C D E

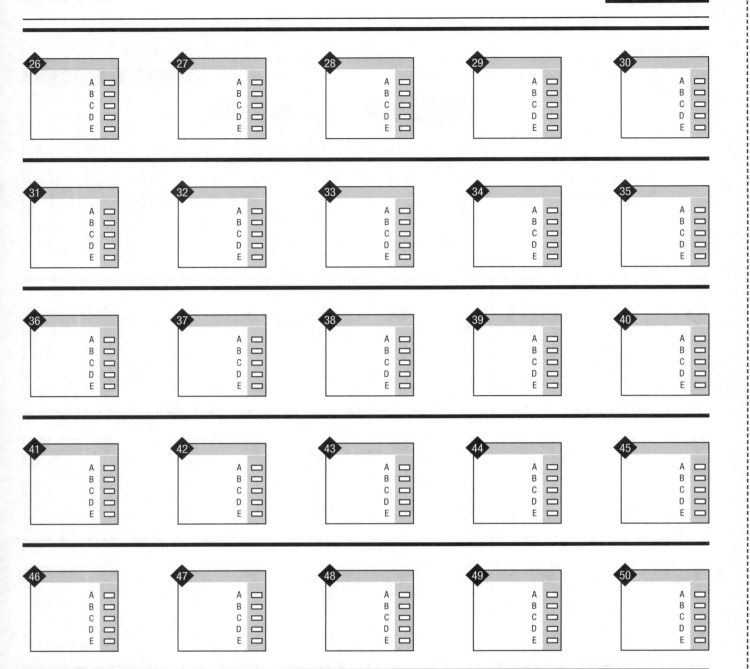

ENGLISH TEST PAPER

Pupil's Name

Date of Test

School Name

DATE OF BIRTH		
Day	Month	Year

PUPIL NUMBER	SCHOOL NUMBER

Pupil Number columns:
[0] [0] [0] [0] [0] [0]
[1] [1] [1] [1] [1] [1]
[2] [2] [2] [2] [2] [2]
[3] [3] [3] [3] [3] [3]
[4] [4] [4] [4] [4] [4]
[5] [5] [5] [5] [5] [5]
[6] [6] [6] [6] [6] [6]
[7] [7] [7] [7] [7] [7]
[8] [8] [8] [8] [8] [8]
[9] [9] [9] [9] [9] [9]

School Number columns:
[0] [0] [0] [0] [0] [0] [0]
[1] [1] [1] [1] [1] [1] [1]
[2] [2] [2] [2] [2] [2] [2]
[3] [3] [3] [3] [3] [3] [3]
[4] [4] [4] [4] [4] [4] [4]
[5] [5] [5] [5] [5] [5] [5]
[6] [6] [6] [6] [6] [6] [6]
[7] [7] [7] [7] [7] [7] [7]
[8] [8] [8] [8] [8] [8] [8]
[9] [9] [9] [9] [9] [9] [9]

Please mark like this ⊟.

Day: [0] [0] / [1] [1] / [2] [2] / [3] [3] / [4] / [5] / [6] / [7] / [8] / [9]

Month: January, February, March, April, May, June, July, August, September, October, November, December

Year: 2007, 2008, 2009, 2010, 2011, 2012, 2013, 2014, 2015, 2016, 2017, 2018

The Signalman

Questions 1–25, each with options A, B, C, D, E.

1. A B C D E
2. A B C D E
3. A B C D E
4. A B C D E
5. A B C D E
6. A B C D E
7. A B C D E
8. A B C D E
9. A B C D E
10. A B C D E
11. A B C D E
12. A B C D E
13. A B C D E
14. A B C D E
15. A B C D E
16. A B C D E
17. A B C D E
18. A B C D E
19. A B C D E
20. A B C D E
21. A B C D E
22. A B C D E
23. A B C D E
24. A B C D E
25. A B C D E

Spelling

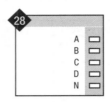
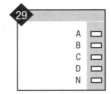

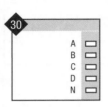
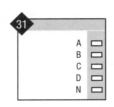

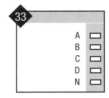

Punctuation

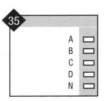

Grammar

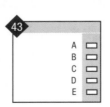

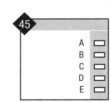

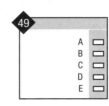

Pupil's Name

School Name

Date of Test

PUPIL NUMBER

[0]	[0]	[0]	[0]	[0]	[0]
[1]	[1]	[1]	[1]	[1]	[1]
[2]	[2]	[2]	[2]	[2]	[2]
[3]	[3]	[3]	[3]	[3]	[3]
[4]	[4]	[4]	[4]	[4]	[4]
[5]	[5]	[5]	[5]	[5]	[5]
[6]	[6]	[6]	[6]	[6]	[6]
[7]	[7]	[7]	[7]	[7]	[7]
[8]	[8]	[8]	[8]	[8]	[8]
[9]	[9]	[9]	[9]	[9]	[9]

SCHOOL NUMBER

[0]	[0]	[0]	[0]	[0]	[0]	[0]
[1]	[1]	[1]	[1]	[1]	[1]	[1]
[2]	[2]	[2]	[2]	[2]	[2]	[2]
[3]	[3]	[3]	[3]	[3]	[3]	[3]
[4]	[4]	[4]	[4]	[4]	[4]	[4]
[5]	[5]	[5]	[5]	[5]	[5]	[5]
[6]	[6]	[6]	[6]	[6]	[6]	[6]
[7]	[7]	[7]	[7]	[7]	[7]	[7]
[8]	[8]	[8]	[8]	[8]	[8]	[8]
[9]	[9]	[9]	[9]	[9]	[9]	[9]

DATE OF BIRTH

Day		Month		Year	
[0]	[0]	January	▢	2007	▢
[1]	[1]	February	▢	2008	▢
[2]	[2]	March	▢	2009	▢
[3]	[3]	April	▢	2010	▢
	[4]	May	▢	2011	▢
	[5]	June	▢	2012	▢
	[6]	July	▢	2013	▢
	[7]	August	▢	2014	▢
	[8]	September	▢	2015	▢
	[9]	October	▢	2016	▢
		November	▢	2017	▢
		December	▢	2018	▢

Please mark like this ⊢.

EXAMPLE — A B C D E

1 2 3 4 5 6 — A B C D E

EXAMPLE — A B C D E

7 8 9 10 11 12 — A B C D E

13 14 15 16 17 18 — A B C D E

EXAMPLE — A B C D E

19 20 21 22 23 24 — A B C D E

EXAMPLE — A B C D E

25 26 27 28 29 30 — A B C D E

31 — A B C D E

EXAMPLE — A B C D E

32 33 34 35 36 37 — A B C D E

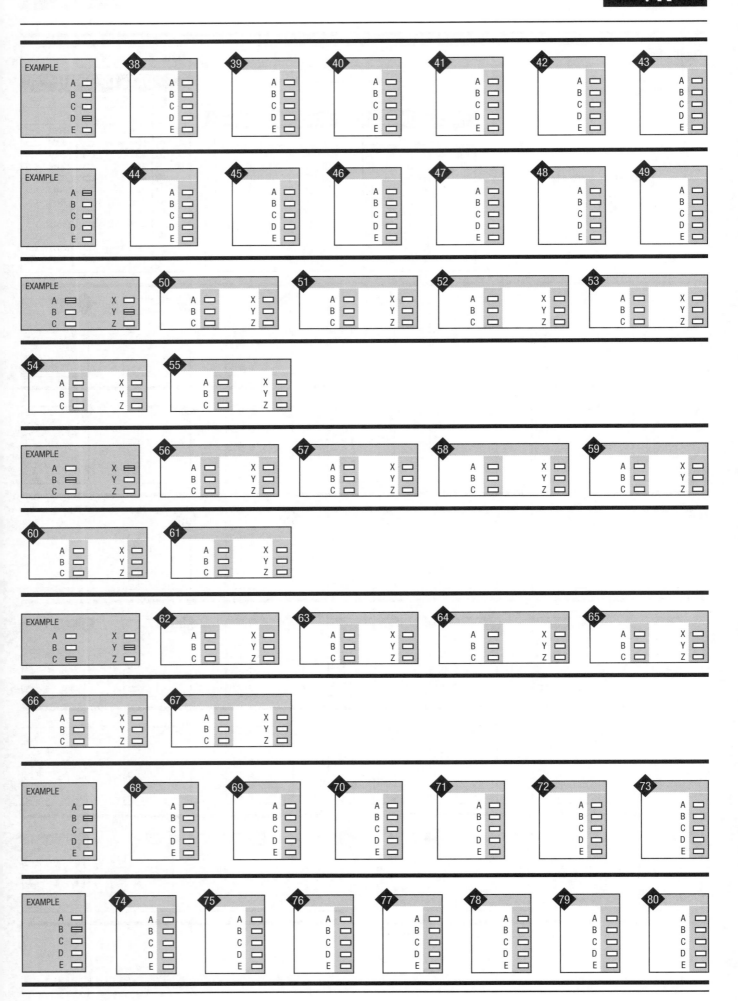

Pupil's Name		Date of Test

School Name	

PUPIL NUMBER

[0]	[0]	[0]	[0]	[0]	[0]
[1]	[1]	[1]	[1]	[1]	[1]
[2]	[2]	[2]	[2]	[2]	[2]
[3]	[3]	[3]	[3]	[3]	[3]
[4]	[4]	[4]	[4]	[4]	[4]
[5]	[5]	[5]	[5]	[5]	[5]
[6]	[6]	[6]	[6]	[6]	[6]
[7]	[7]	[7]	[7]	[7]	[7]
[8]	[8]	[8]	[8]	[8]	[8]
[9]	[9]	[9]	[9]	[9]	[9]

SCHOOL NUMBER

[0]	[0]	[0]	[0]	[0]	[0]	[0]
[1]	[1]	[1]	[1]	[1]	[1]	[1]
[2]	[2]	[2]	[2]	[2]	[2]	[2]
[3]	[3]	[3]	[3]	[3]	[3]	[3]
[4]	[4]	[4]	[4]	[4]	[4]	[4]
[5]	[5]	[5]	[5]	[5]	[5]	[5]
[6]	[6]	[6]	[6]	[6]	[6]	[6]
[7]	[7]	[7]	[7]	[7]	[7]	[7]
[8]	[8]	[8]	[8]	[8]	[8]	[8]
[9]	[9]	[9]	[9]	[9]	[9]	[9]

Please mark like this ⊢.

DATE OF BIRTH

Day		Month		Year	
[0]	[0]	January	☐	2007	☐
[1]	[1]	February	☐	2008	☐
[2]	[2]	March	☐	2009	☐
[3]	[3]	April	☐	2010	☐
	[4]	May	☐	2011	☐
	[5]	June	☐	2012	☐
	[6]	July	☐	2013	☐
	[7]	August	☐	2014	☐
	[8]	September	☐	2015	☐
	[9]	October	☐	2016	☐
		November	☐	2017	☐
		December	☐	2018	☐

SECTION 1

SECTION 2

SECTION 3

  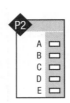

SECTION 4

SECTION 5